Doing His Bit

Doing His Bit
A Shetland Soldier in the Great War

Robert M. Greig

Edited by Alex Cluness

The Shetland Times Ltd.,
Lerwick.
2014

Doing His Bit: A Shetland Soldier in the Great War.

ISBN 978-1-898852-46-9

First published in collected form by The Shetland Times Ltd, 1999.
Reprinted, 2014

Publisher's Note: The date of original publication of each article in *The Shetland Times* is given under each chapter heading.

Cover design by The Stafford Partnership, Shetland.

Front cover photo: Robert M. Greig.
Back cover photo: Robert M. Greig with his daughter

British Library Cataloguing-in-Publication Data
A catalogue record for this book is available from the British Library.

Printed and published by
The Shetland Times Ltd.,
Gremista, Lerwick,
Shetland. ZE1 0PX.

CONTENTS

ILLUSTRATIONS

1. The Bull-ring at Étaples. "a city founded on sand". (Q33342).

2. A Church parade behind the lines on the Western Front. (Q3055)

3. A Seaforth Highlanders Lewis Gun post, 23rd October, 1917 (HU 75116).

4. Stretcher bearers at Ypres: "the trackless waste, full of pitfalls and dangers...". (Q7014).

5. Ypres, 1917: "Nearer a picture of hell than any mortal had yet conceived". (Q11679)

6. Exhausted Seaforth Highlanders Stretcher Bearers, 29th August, 1918. (Q7014)

7. The 2nd Battalion Seaforth Highlanders form the Guard of Honour, 25th February, 1918. (HU 75116)

8. Seaforth Highlanders patrol moving forward, 29th August, 1918. (Q7009)

Photographs reproduced with the permission of the The Trustees of the Imperial War Museum, London, reference numbers shown.

ABBREVIATIONS

C. O. Commanding Officer

D. C. M. Distinguished Conduct Medal

M. O. Medical Officer

N. C. O. Non-commissioned Officer. For example, a corporal.

O. C. Officer Commanding

Q. M. S. Quartermaster Sergeant

R. A. M. C. Royal Army Medical Corps

R. F. A. Royal Field Artillery

R. G. A. Royal Garrison Artillery

R. H. A. Royal Horse Artillery

R. S. M. Regimental Sergeant Major

W. A. A. C. Women's Army Auxiliary Corps

W. O. Warrant Officer – a senior N. C. O., e.g. R. S. M., Q. M. S.

Y. M. C. A. Young Men's Christian Association

INTRODUCTION

ROBERT MORRISON GREIG was born in 1892. His father, Peter Greig, was editor and joint proprietor of *The Shetland Times*. After his time in the Anderson High School, Lerwick, where he won several prizes for essay writing, the young Robert Greig went to work for his father in 1908. He trained as a reporter and then proceeded to Edinburgh, where he did a nine month course in a shorthand school. He then spent a short while law reporting in Edinburgh before returning to Lerwick to take up his post as assistant reporter at *The Shetland Times*. In 1916, he enlisted in the Great War. On his return, between January and August 1920, he wrote a series of articles for the paper on his war experiences. These were entitled *Doing His Bit: What It Meant*.

The summary facts of Greig's war career are there, but a precise chronology is difficult to achieve. Great War research does breed an obsession to put dates, places, names and numbers on everything, but sometimes this just isn't possible, and even inconclusive researches can take years. For example, an enquiry at the Ministry of Defence discovered that Robert Greig's service records were among those destroyed in the Blitz. Added to this, as he says himself, his diaries were lost during the German advance in March 1918. These two facts make it difficult to be exact about Greig's war.

With the Shetland soldiers of the Great War, the starting block is always *Shetland's Roll of Honour and Roll of Service*. Robert Greig's entry is as follows:

> R.M. GREIG, Corporal, 5th Cameron Highlanders and 2nd Seaforth Highlanders, ex R.A.M.C. Queen's Lane

It seems that Greig enlisted in 1916, and after a period training on the mainland, he was included in a draft for the East, possibly bound for Mesopotamia, Egypt or Salonika. It is likely that he was part of the Royal Army Medical Corps at this time, as the 2nd Seaforths and 5th Camerons were in France. After the dramatic sinking of the troopship he was travelling on, Greig returned to France and then back to Britain. He spent more time training on the mainland before joining a draft bound for the 2nd Seaforth Highlanders in France. Before leaving for the front line, he spent yet another training period at the infamous Bull-Ring at Etaples.[1] On arriving at the front it seems that he was sent straight into action in The Third Battle of Ypres or, as it is now more commonly known, Passchendaele. After this action he spent the winter in the line near Arras. He then participated in the retreat following the German offensive of March 1918 and the consequent Allied advances. It is likely that he was still a part of the 2nd Seaforths at this time, as they were stationed at Saulzoir, near Valenciennes, at the Armistice, which corresponds with his

---

[1] The Bull Ring was the name given to the parade ground at the British Army's main training depot in France, at Étaples. Conditions were brutal.

account. He may then have been drafted into the 5th Camerons as a Corporal in the Army of Occupation. He was also awarded the Croix de Guerre at some point during the war, and there is a suggestion that he was attached to the French army at some time. He was demobilised in November 1919.

* * * * *

In his definitive account of the Battle of Arras in 1917, *Cheerful Sacrifice*, Jonathan Nicholls captures vividly one of the remarkable stories of the First World War:

In the late afternoon of 22nd February, 1917, while holed up in a frozen trench just south of the German-held ruins of Petit Miraumont, Lieutenant Frank Lucas of the 7th Royal West Kents, suspicious at a strange lack of enemy activity from the trenches opposite, clambered up on the slippery firestep and peered into the gloom. Squinting through field glasses only served to amplify the murk. He could not see a thing. Scrambling quickly over the parapet he decided to take a closer look. The 55th Infantry Brigade was holding the whole of the 18th Division's front at the head of the shell-torn Ancre Valley[2] and this was not normally a quiet sector; Lucas was curious as to what the Germans might be up to. Cautiously he advanced along the battered West Miraumont road until he came to the hedges of rusty barbed wire that lay in front of the enemy trench, and, even more cautiously, picked his way through the steel briars, crawled up to the parapet and peered down. To his amazement he saw that the trench was empty. On the left he saw a lone German soldier climb out of the trench, stand up and run swiftly back towards the ruins of the village. The enemy had abandoned their trenches.

Slithering breathlessly in the cold air back into his own lines, Lucas immediately reported his findings to his dubious senior officers. No patrols could be sent out during the night to confirm Lucas's story, because of the danger of British artillery shelling the German front trenches; but at 5am the following morning Lucas obtained permission to go out again, this time taking with him Lieutenant Francis Lewin. The two officers, with revolvers at the ready, then crept along Crest Trench for several hundred yards, meeting no one. There was no doubt about it—the Germans had gone.

---

[2] The Ancre valley was a place of bitter memory for many of the Shetland Soldiers. Members of the Territorial "Shetland Companies" took part in various actions on the Somme on 13th November, 1916, including the attack on Beaumont Hamel. Within a fortnight Shetlanders were faced with the appalling news that 16 of the boys had been killed and 22 wounded. The date marks one of the saddest days in the history of Shetland in the Twentieth Century.

Lucas and Lewin had uncovered the result, in their own sector, of what is now known as Operation Alberich[3]. In order to shorten their line by twenty-five miles, and release thirteen divisions of badly needed soldiers, the Germans had planned and executed the most extraordinary tactical withdrawal. They had retreated to the formidable Siegfried Stellung, a vast network of reinforced concrete blockhouses, machine gun posts and bunkers, disguised or buried deep within layers of earth, and stretching from Arras to Rheims. After a misunderstanding with a German prisoner, this formidable obstacle would be known to the British as The Hindenburg Line.

Severely weakened after the horrific Verdun, and anticipating further British attacks, the German Army could see no alternative to giving ground. So they retreated, leaving chaos and destruction behind them—levelling houses, destroying trees, fouling wells, planting booby traps. Incredibly, they achieved all this without the Allies realising and, even more astoundingly, early intelligence from the British that the enemy were retreating didn't even force the French Commander Nivelle to alter the plans for his disastrous offensive of April 1917.

When the allies finally did advance it was too late to catch the Germans in the open. Like the amazing evacuation of Gallipoli in 1915, an army had disappeared into the night. Now they sheltered behind a fortress line of brutal complexity. Even the village of Serre,[4] the scene of such carnage during the Battle of the Somme, had been abandoned. In their new defensive positions, the Germans waited. When Lucas and Lewin dropped into Crest Trench, they went down in history as two of the men who blew the whistle on one of the most successful operations of the war. As they stood there, staring at each other in amazement, they were the only soldiers in the German trenches for miles.

There is something haunting about this story: the single German soldier disappearing from the trench, the line empty in the darkness of a late afternoon. Perhaps it's because it's easy to allow this empty trench to become symbolic. Bluntly, as we near the end of the Twentieth Century, very few of the Great War soldiers are still living, so the trenches are empty. The image of a "lone German soldier", disappearing into the cold haze, the idea of crawling across No Man's Land to find the enemy lines abandoned, has such a bleached, dreamlike

---

3   Jonathan Nicholls: "The withdrawal...has become known as Operation Alberich, after the malicious dwarf of the Nibelung Saga, although Alberich was, strictly speaking, just the name of the sector south of St Quentin, facing the French. In view of the awesome difficulty of pulling back an army under the noses of the enemy, Operation Alberich proved to be one of the most brilliant German operations of the war."

4   Serre was another name of evil for the Shetland soldier. In the attack on the 13th November, 1916, the last gasp of the Battle of the Somme, a number of Shetlanders were killed at Serre. Robert Coutts of Lerwick was killed in this battle. He is buried in the Varennes Military Cemetery, France. D.W. Anderson of Hoolsgarth, Lerwick was also among the Shetlanders who died. He is buried in Queens Cemetery, France. The inscription on his grave reads, "For Freedom". Robert Coutts's brother John was killed almost to the day the following year, on the 20th November, 1917. He is buried in Orival Wood cemetery, Flesquieres, France.

quality, that it is deeply poignant. If in our mind we blur this empty trench of 1917 with the empty preserved trenches of the Newfoundland Park,[5] for example, past and present merge as one. The duality is striking: the trenches really are empty now, the men who fought in them missing. Although it sticks in the throat to suggest it, the Great War may be only one generation away from becoming just another war.

John Keegan's masterly *The Face of Battle*, already one of the most striking studies of the carnage on the Somme, in some sense anticipated this inevitable assimilation—the book is a study of the experience of war, with the Somme being only one essay in a series that includes chapters on Agincourt, Waterloo and the future of war; like the endless transmutations of Peter Ackroyd's *Hawksmoor*, it's hard not to ponder this and imagine great cycles at work. It is no great leap from such thinking to see Lucas's fleeing Boche become as one with the last surviving soldiers of the First World War, on both sides: a merry few diminishing yearly, turning out for the relentless anniversaries, Lest we forget. The trenches of the Newfoundland Park are still there for us to see, but the grass has grown over them. Gradually they become part of a history that is past, rather than living. They are a tourist attraction. Geoff Dyer captures this uneasy context-shifting well in his exceptional *The Missing of the Somme:*

> We arrive there on a November morning. The sky is armistice-white. The trenches are still preserved but without the barbed wire—removed, finally, because sheep kept getting tangled up in it—the grass-covered shell-holes make the place look like a particularly difficult golf course.

In the past, when the historian of the Great War needed information, those who were there could tell the tale. Even yet, this is still possible. Indeed, with the destruction of many of the military records of Great War soldiers in the Blitz, the individual soldier's story, as opposed to the broader military picture, often had to be saved in this way, through the tireless efforts of such committed individuals as Lyn MacDonald, Martin Middlebrook and Denis Winter—writers who allowed the soldiers to speak for themselves. As the century draws to a close we realise how indebted we really are to these historians for their dedication. Five million British soldiers saw active service in the First World

---

5   The Newfoundland Memorial Park is an 80 acre site of preserved trenches bought by Newfoundland after the war. It covers the area held by the Royal Newfoundland Regiment on the day of their tragic advance on the 1st July, 1916, the first day of the Battle of the Somme. 710 soldiers of the regiment were killed.

For visitors to the battlefields, three books are essential:
Coombs, Rose B., M.B.E., *Before Endeavours Fade*, After the Battle, London, 1994.
Holt, Tony and Valmai, *Battlefields of The First World War*, Pavilion, London, 1995.
Middlebrook, Martin and Mary, *The Somme Battlefields*, Penguin, London, 1994.
Also extremely valuable are the *Battleground Europe* guidebooks which deal with individual battles and actions in greater detail. They are published by Pen and Sword Books Ltd.

War, but they didn't all have the means to find access to publishers, like Sassoon or Graves. Some did sneak through to publication, like Coppard and Hiscock, and in his bibliography of memoirs cited in *Death's Men*, Denis Winter records 227 publications. Nevertheless, the great majority of soldiers had no voice. Historians like Macdonald, however, were determined to listen to the stories of these men from the trenches, to record their memories. In the research for *They Called It Passchendaele* alone, Macdonald interviewed more than 600 soldiers. In another hundred years historians will turn to such works of social history with an astonished gratitude.

Nonetheless, as "Current Topics"[6], Robert Greig's co-contributor to *The Shetland Times*, would say, all this is digression. Like Nicholls's last soldier retreating into the mists, we now have to face the fact that the living voices of the Great War are, to paraphrase a song about Old Soldiers, simply fading away. Even a soldier who was fifteen, and some were, in 1916, will be 99 as the century ends.[7] The men who knew Delville Wood, Passchendaele Ridge and Beaumont Hamel are nearly all gone. The sadness that accompanies this realisation is unbearable for those who are closely linked to the war by immediate generations, who knew their grandfather was there, for example, or their father. The time to learn from the boys of the trenches has all but gone. History repeatedly delivers the same harsh lesson: ask before it's too late.

Although a staple in schools, through the study of poets like Owen and Sassoon and the constant analysis of battles like the Somme in History classrooms, for future generations the Ypres described by Greig in this book will grow ever distant. Our historical consciousness of the Great War is on the verge of a new era. Battlefield archaeology, for instance, is no longer the preserve of the foolhardy collector, roaming the fields for shrapnel balls, or a rusty shell casing: real excavations take place—at Messines, for example. It is astonishing to watch, but as we see old trench networks and tunnels rediscovered on television documentaries, rum jars carefully brushed from the earth like Roman pottery, it is impossible not to feel the ebb of history

---

6 'Current Topics', a regular outspoken column in *The Shetland Times,* may have been written by Greig himself in 1920, although the authors apparently changed. On the war, in the column of August 7, 1920, the peremptory style of 'Current Topics' is strangely familiar:

...In the period 1914-1920 much had happened. The world and civilisation had been shaken to their foundations. Men had been called from the fields, the workshop, the counting house - from all branches of industrial pursuits, in fact, and put in uniform, were sent forth to endure hardship and suffer and die. For what? Let us get clear of cant of "love of country" and "cause of freedom", and come down to the materialistic aspect of the matter—for a shilling a day! And at home? A government doing its utmost to create new departments, filling them with pampered favourites at fabulous salaries...

7 Private J. Condon of the Royal Irish Regiment was 14 when he died at Ypres on the 24th of May 1915. Lieutenant Henry "Harry" Webber of the 7th South Lancs. was the oldest soldier to die on the Western Front. He was 68.

reclaiming the Soldiers of the Great War. It's hard not to be despondent, to feel that the men themselves have finally fallen silent.

However, if history tells us one thing, it's to never assume that any interpretation of the past is cut and dried. Amazingly, unexpected voices from the Great War still spring up, heckling like rowdy Jocks at some vin blanc/plonc fuelled Estaminet entertainment behind the lines. They are still singing in boxes of faded letters cornered in an attic, in the papyrus pages of regional newspapers, in second-hand bookshops, on the backs of postcards with the names of towns scored out by the censor, in the yellow hieroglyphs of microfiche—they are hidden in the informal attic archives of a nation. Voices break through all the time, we only have to listen. Robert Greig's *Doing His Bit* is a startling example.

Like Macdonald, Winter and Middlebrook, with their passionate concern for their sources, staff at the Shetland Archives found Greig's testimony in *The Shetland Times* and realised immediately that it was an important document. Assistant Archivist Angus Johnson discovered the articles and the late Roy Gronneberg typed up the manuscript. Brian Smith, the County Archivist, recognised its value for publication. John J. Graham was the next to spot the merit of the articles. *Doing His Bit* had marched back from the empty front line.

* * * * *

After the war Robert Greig got on with his life. Like so many survivors, however, the burden of experience must have been heavy. The image of grim faced men who didn't talk about it might be a cliché, but it's probably fairly accurate. Perhaps over a dram or two they would relive their days in the trenches but generally, it seems, only with someone who had served "over there", who knew how terrible it had been. In short, with those who understood. This gulf in understanding between those who went and those who didn't is a recurring feature in Western Front literature. Like an Up-Helly-A' squad there was a bond between men from all different walks of life, who in the course of a year might hardly meet at all, but on getting together share something important between them as a unit—their own history, mythology, language, sense of humour. Of course, the Up-Helly-A' comparison is hopelessly inadequate, but its obvious shortcomings merely help to emphasise the simple fact that those who weren't there can never understand (Up-Helly-A' is a "fire festival" held in Lerwick every January). True empathy, when it comes to the slaughter of the Western Front, is virtually a forlorn endeavour.

Despite their usual reticence on the subject, the veterans would still take a keen interest in any new information on their war. The Great War series of the 1960s, for those who had access to the television, would have been compulsive viewing. Here, it seemed, was their side of the story. They also read new accounts of the war with an insider's zeal for accuracy, and new fiction, one imagines, with permanently raised eyebrows. They might have talked about it openly only rarely, but it was still very much a part of their lives, and on occasion, often prompted by curious grandchildren who recognised no taboo subject, they did talk. They each had stock stories for those who were interested—lice, frozen kilts, mud, eating raw onions. One Shetland soldier recalled vividly the bare backside of his battalion cook disappearing into battle —he had no kilt under his apron; another the ribbing from his chums about a "sweetheart" when a single red rose arrived from his sister. These were the stories they liked to tell; it was just that very few of them wanted to reveal the deeper emotions that seemed to stake them to the ground. They were men who harboured memories of experiences beyond the grasp of those who weren't there.

To some it may seem unbelievable, but many men of the younger generation of the Twenties, who had been too young to fight, felt a pang of envy for these remarkable men from the trenches—just as the young Robert Greig is keen to experience Ypres, despite the tales of horror he hears from a Shetlander on a train journey. Geoff Dyer recounts the post-war blues of two significant figures of that era:

> Christopher Isherwood, who was born in 1904, the year after Orwell, recalls that "we young writers of the middle twenties were all suffering, more or less subconsciously, from a feeling of shame that we hadn't been old enough to take part in the European war". The war for Isherwood was a subject of "all-consuming morbid interest', 'a complex of terrors and longings". Longing could sometimes outweigh terror as the Orwell-Isherwood generation "became conscious of the vastness of the experience they had missed". Hence the fascination of the Spanish Civil War, Orwell goes on, "was that it was so like the Great War".

It was difficult, however, for these returning men of vast experience to reconcile their life in the war with their life back home in Shetland—working for the county, or fishing, teaching or working for the customs, working for the papers, not finding any work at all. Even in Shetland it was possible for a veteran of the Western Front to die with no money, without a proper roof over his head, face first in the Lerwick mud. Understandably, some had no desire to reconcile their two existences whatsoever, and decided that the war was never going to be a part of the lives of the people around them, except perhaps as an example of an abomination which should never be allowed again. There were often no homes for heroes and certainly none of the counselling of the 1990s to ease their return to civvy street, so the men simply had to "get on". The long-term social effects of their return, and the implications for succeeding generations, will no doubt be scrutinised to a greater degree in the future. In some senses, thanks to the media and Hollywood, this process has happened in America at a faster pace with the Vietnam War.

* * * * *

In 1920, like many Great War veterans, Robert Greig began to write—to put down for the readers of *The Shetland Times* what he describes as "the edges of things". He seemed motivated by the desire to cut through the grand talk of the day, the whitewash about gallant sacrifice bringing the world to peace and liberty, etc. It was a similar sense of distaste that fuelled the despair of Wilfred Owen; the same frustration that Paul Baumer feels when he is in the beer garden in *All Quiet on the Western Front*:

> The head-master with the steel watch-chain wants to have at least the whole of Belgium, the coal areas of France, and a slice of Russia. He produces reasons why we must have them and is quite inflexible until at last the others give in to him. Then he begins to expound where in France the break-through must come, and turns to me: "Now, shove ahead a bit out there with your everlasting trench warfare —Smash through the johnnies and then there will be peace."
> I reply that in our opinion a break-through may not be possible. The enemy have too many reserves. Besides, the war may be rather different from what people think.

What really strikes the reader of *Doing His Bit* is the voice of Robert Greig that comes through—the voice of a writer steadfastly determined not to elevate himself above those he fought with, or against, in any way. It is a stance that can be picked up in many accounts of the war. On the few occasions he does draw any distinction he is immediately repentant, heartbreakingly so in the tragic description of a dying pal who offers Greig his last cigarette. There is a loyalty of spirit that is intensely moving. The poet Ewart Alan MacKintosh was a soldier in the 5th Seaforth Highlanders. MacKintosh's most famous poem is 'In Memoriam, Private D. Sutherland', the penultimate stanza of which reveals exactly the kind of loyalty Greig expresses himself:

> Oh, never will I forget you,
> My men that trusted me,
> More my sons than your fathers',
> For they could only see
> The little helpless babies
> And the young men in their pride.
> They could not see you dying,
> And hold you when you died.

MacKintosh was in the same Battalion as Karl Manson, the son of Thomas Manson of *The Shetland News*. They may well have known each other. After recovering from a wound on the Somme, MacKintosh turned down a "cushy" training job to return to the lads. Posted to the 4th Seaforths he was killed at the Battle of Cambrai. Karl Manson was also killed in 1917, at the Battle of Arras.

Greig's identification with the soldiers as one great unit is emphasised by his insistence on using the language of the troops. With tell tale inverted commas he emphasises how the men of the trenches were a band of brothers even in their vocabulary. He speaks of soldiers who have "gone west", the church parade as a "wash out", an attack as a "stunt", billets as "cushy". There is even occasionally that tone of understatement that characterises several reminiscences of the war—the working party is "fed up", the blood from the bayonet attack is "not pleasant". 55 years later, in his groundbreaking work *The Great War and Modern Memory* Paul Fussell is exceptional on the language structures of the trenches.[8] In the chapter 'O, What a Literary War', the sense of language as a uniting force emerges clearly:

> The constant meeting and passing of marching units on the roads generated a large repertory of road humour based on musical and literary patterns of orderly insult. Passing a well-known battalion, a marcher would shout out "Bugger!" His colleagues would take this as the first two notes of the Colonel Bogey March, and after a suitable pause would sing out the rest of the melody: "—the Worcestershires!"

"Indescribable" and "horror" are two words which often crop up, separately or together, in accounts of the Western Front battlefields, and this is probably because they were the most accurate words to use. Even those who were there would later find it barely believable that they had witnessed what they did. They refer often to an inability to capture just how diabolical their surroundings were, and Greig does the same, but his description of Ypres, his first taste of battle, is powerful nonetheless. It is clear, both from the placing in the chronology of articles, and from the tone of the writing, that Passchendaele was a defining experience of Greig's war:

> These trenches—lines of shell-holes and scraped up earth—were, when I was there, in a nice, slimy condition. If one touched anything, and one could not but be without doing so, some of the mud stuck, and soon one had a large collection of Ypres mud all over one's person. To add to the pleasantness of the prospect, all around were dead men in all stages of decomposition, and even bits of men were strewn here and there. Some of these had never been buried, some had been, but their last rest had been disturbed and a shell had unearthed the body or part of it. After wholesome training camps of Britain and a wholesome base depot, this sort of thing came as an unpleasant shock, and my constant wish from then on was that peace might come swiftly, or that I might get a "Blighty one" and get out of it all. To add to the general unpleasantness there was a continual growl of artillery and the rapping of machine-guns, with their constant concert of whining shells, and hissing bullets, a fearsome din concluding with nerve-rending reports as the shells burst.

---

8   Paul Fussell knows war well. *The Great War and Modern Memory* is dedicated "To the memory of Technical Sergeant Edward Keith Hudson, ASN 36548772 Co. F, 410th Infantry, Killed beside me in France, March 15, 1945."

Even getting to the front line was nearly impossible. The Ypres battleground that Robert Greig knew is brought horrifically to life in the observations of a company commander of the Royal Warwickshire Regiment, moving across the battlefield at much the same time[9]:

> For the first few miles we moved along a single duck-board track laid down on a vast sea of mud. Movement was difficult and slow, although separate up and down tracks were in use. By the time we had reached the end of the duck-boards night had fallen and guides from the front line met us to lead us as best as they could on solid ground between the maze of water-filled shell-holes. Into these many men fell and got soaked in the foul water, and were fortunate indeed if they were seen and saved from almost certain drowning, weighed down as they were by their heavy equipment. Picture the puny efforts of a small fly to cross the pudding basin full of batter and you have some idea of the hopelessness of the man who has missed the track and become bogged in this appalling mud which appeared to have no solid bottom. A party of 'A' company men passing up to the front line found such a man bogged to above the knees. The united efforts of four of them with rifles beneath his armpits, made not the slightest impression, and to dig, even if shovels had been available, would be impossible, for there was no foothold. Duty compelled them to move on up to the line, and when two days later they passed down that way the wretched fellow was still there; but only his head was now visible and he was raving mad.

If Robert Greig was in the 2nd Seaforths at the time of the action at Ypres he describes, and there is enough evidence to suggest this, the attack he was involved in has become known as the Battle of Broodseinde, October 4, 1917. Chris McCarthy:

> Temperature 60 F; overcast. Rainfall: 4.6mm.
>
> 10 Brigade, attacking at 6 a.m. with the 2nd Seaforth Highlanders and with the 3/10th Middlesex in support, crossed the Laudetbeek Marsh and lost direction. The Brigade came under machine-gun fire from its left flank. The Seaforths, reinforced by some Middlesex, achieved their first objective, a line on the road on the far side of 19 Metre Hill. After pausing for an hour they continued the attack but, still under machine-gun fire, abandoned it and consolidated.

Sir Douglas Haig thought the day went well:

> To-day was a very important success and we had great good fortune in that the enemy had concentrated such a large number of Divisions just at the moment of our attack with the very intense Artillery barrages.
>
> Over 3,000 prisoners and six guns are already reported captured.

---

9   From Bill C.A., The 15th Battalion The Royal Warwickshire Regiment in the Great War (Birmingham, 1932), quoted in J.H. Johnston's *Stalemate!*

It was a day the Germans called "The Black Day of October Fourth". It seemed that a breakthrough had been made, although Leon Wolff is sceptical:

> On the other side of the hill, British comments were joyous ... Even more cheery than usual, Charteris[10] thought that the Germans had been so mangled that they possessed "few more available reserves." He ... exclaimed, "Now we have them on the run—get up the cavalry!" The Australian official historian writes: "An overwhelming blow had been struck, and both sides knew it." For the London Press Philip Gibbs reported, "It had been a bad defeat for them and they did not hide their despair." British officers claimed a record number of dead Germans littering the captured area and New Zealanders spoke of unusually heavy casualties dealt the enemy and boasted that their division alone had taken 1,159 captives. General Plumer called it "the greatest victory since the Marne".
>
> All this seems to indicate a triumph beyond argument or carping, despite the deteriorating weather.
>
> Yet an examination of the map shows that the physical gains were even smaller than in the two previous attacks. The ex-towns of Gravenstafel and Poelcapelle were captured (the latter not entirely), the remnants of Polygon Wood were occupied, Broodseinde was taken, and so was the remaining half of Zonnebeke village. Averaging out the gains over the entire front from Tower Hamlets to the Ypres-Staden railroad, one learns that the dividend was some 700 yards. The price of this investment was nearly 26,000 casualties, half of whom were killed or missing.

Philip Warner adds the soldier's perspective. Desmond Allhusen, 60th Rifles:

> Then some men in the middle were blown off the path by a shell. By the time they had picked themselves up the front part of the platoon had gone. Here there was heavy shelling and wounded men were lying everywhere. It was an awful pandemonium, something like the medieval idea of hell, pitch dark apart from the evil flashes of bursting shells, screams, groans and sobs, men writhing in the mud, men trying to walk and falling down again and everywhere figures scurrying like lost souls, backwards and forwards, blaspheming and imploring someone to tell them the way. It seems that when a man turns his back to the front he is on the road to panic and when his mind and body have reached breaking-point the road is not so long.

---

[10] General John Charteris was Sir Douglas Haig's Chief of Intelligence. Haig's Chief of Staff was Launcelot Kiggell, who reportedly wept when he saw for the first time at close quarters the Passchendaele battlefield, exclaiming, "Good God, did we really send men to fight in this?"

One of the most powerful attempts to get at the meaning of Ypres for the British soldier appears in Stephen Graham's *The Challenge of the Dead* and describes the town after the war:

> This Ypres is a terrible place still. There is no life when night comes on but tavern life. Those who live and work here have lost their sense of proportion. They are out of focus somehow. "You lookin' for dead soldiers," says a Flemish woman to you with a glaring stare, wondering if you are one of the exhumers. Death and the ruins completely outweigh the living. One is tilted out of time by the huge weight on the other end of the plank, and it would be easy to imagine someone who had no insoluble ties killing himself here, drawn by the lodestone of death. There is a pull from the other world, a drag on the heart and spirit. One is ashamed to be alive. You try to sleep in a little bed in a cubicle with tiny doll's house window. You listen to a drunken company down below singing, "Mademoiselle, have you got any rum?" A French couple enter the room next door, smacking one another's hips and confounding one another with coarse violent laughter—that is the light end of the plank. Then night ensues, the real night, breathless and sepulchral, the night which belongs to all lost hopes and ended lives and wearinesses.

As an insight into the details of war as experienced by individuals, as opposed to a generalised overview, *Doing His Bit* is extremely graphic. Take, for example, the chapter on bayonet fighting, and the focus on the senses: the touch, the sight, the smell, the noise of the bayonet fight. It is vivid and unforgettable. The aftermath is horrendous. Like Macbeth, "Will all great Neptune's oceans wash this blood clean from my hand?":

> Needless to say, the bayonet in use soon became very messy, and this mess soon affected the rifle, so that it had that sticky, greasy feeling blood usually has. One's clothes too, already sticky with blood, became spattered with blood, and the smell of blood pervaded everything. At the time of fighting that did not affect one to any great extent, but as soon as it was over, the effect was ghastly. One was literally overwhelmed with disgust. The blood caked to one's rifle and hands, and there was no chance of a wash. One had to eat with human blood on one's clothes, and, even after the hands had been rubbed and "scraped", there was blood under and around the fingernails.

Greig's revelations about the bayonet are of great interest to the historian of trench warfare because they are further evidence against the view that the bayonet was rarely used. In Denis Winter's *Death's Men*, an essential text for those interested in life in the trenches, there is strong support for Greig's evidence:

> In battle the twenty-one inch sword bayonet would be added to the rifle...For most of the Great War it was simply an anachronism, useful as a toasting fork, biscuit slicer or intimidator of prisoners. In the confined space of a trench it was as likely

to wound friend as enemy. Attached to a rifle, its additional weight made fire calculations more difficult. General Harper at the time and Brigadier Essame today insist that "no man in the Great War was ever killed by a bayonet unless he had his hands up first." This was not just a matter of clumsiness for, if there was a chance of escape, few would fight at close quarters with cold steel. The imagination was too lively to contemplate coolly a stand-up with bread knives at close quarters. But the memoirs of front-line men gave the lie to the confident assertions of generals. At night, in fog, in a wood or whenever surprise and difficulty of escape coincided, bayonets were used and often. Depth of incision left few survivors, though, if a man was not killed initially, he stood a fair chance of surviving if a dry bandage was applied. Letter-writers describe the sensation of bayoneting as being like inserting a knife point first into butter, the only problem being that of extricating the blade, since skin and muscle closed on the knife. Thus the half twist which men in training were taught.

Or the trick Greig learns from a French soldier "which consisted of engaging the other man's bayonet and thrusting high".

Similarly, Greig describes vividly the nerve shattering effects of the extended bombardment on the front line soldier. He acknowledges the sensory disruption that seemed to affect all but the coolest front line men in these armageddon-like exchanges between the big guns. Only the practised, sternest soldier could judge with any accuracy the various shrieks and whines. In the darkness the sky was lit up with flashes, flares and explosions. Screaming shards of red hot shrapnel would tear a man to pieces as the noise above ground skirled beyond the range of any useful adjective. It is little wonder that the toll on the men under fire was so extreme. Sometimes, the fear would never leave, and old men would leap from their skins when a car backfired on the Esplanade. As always, Denis Winter finds the telling evidence with a forensic intensity:

No one was immune. Some stared at their hands clasped on their knees in a state of catatonic fear. Some hid their heads in their greatcoats in a state of torpor. Others would sit in certain positions, touch particular objects, whistle so many bars of a particular tune to ward evil off with ritual. Some wept; others joked hysterically. But all shook and crawled, white faced in dull endurance, "How long? How long?" men would ask themselves again and again. Men had no choice but to last out, nerves pared to the bone. Griffith[11] described his experience under a barrage. 'After a thunderous crash in our ears, a young boy began to cry for his mother in a thin, boyish voice. "Mam, mam..." He had not been hit but was frightened and crying quietly. Suddenly he started screaming again, screaming for his mother with a wail that seemed older than the world. The men began to mutter uneasily. We shook him and cursed him and even threatened to kill him if he did not stop. The shaking brought him back.

---

11   Griffith, W., the author of *Up to Mametz*, Faber, London, 1931

The account of battle in *Doing His Bit* is intense. Greig talks of the misery waiting in the trench, the moments of complete agony as the bombardment thunders around them. He talks of the relief to be finally moving. When they are finally "over the bags" they find themselves in a maelstrom of bullets and flying shrapnel, "practically every man with a newly lit cigarette in his mouth". Greig's account is vivid:

So we went on, thinned a little, and came to the first line of the enemy. Then we started to run, charged, and shouted, threw a bomb or two, and jumped into the enemy trench. The barbed wire in front had been severely dealt with by the artillery, so that our passing was comparatively easy, and those Germans who did not surrender, considerably bolted, so that we had the trench without a great struggle. Then on again. We came to the second trench and entered it in much the same way, but we were less fortunate here, for we had hardly got into it when the Germans launched a counter-attack in force and promptly drove us out, We had a good number of casualties here before we steadied and went back.

The dreadful human results of such an attack are described with haunting effect by Lyn Macdonald. In this instance, evening on the first day of the Battle of the Somme:

As they neared the wood, between the roar of explosions, behind the sickening gas-soaked mist, in the forefront of the noise that raged at them from every horizon, the small party of the West Yorkshires became aware of another sound. It was like nothing they had ever heard before. Later—and for the rest of his life—Lieutenant Hornshaw was to remember it as a sound that chilled the blood; a nerve scraping noise 'like enormous wet fingers screeching across an enormous pane of glass.' It was coming from the wounded, lying out in No Man's Land. Some screaming, some muttering, some weeping with fear, some calling for help, shouting in delirium, groaning with pain, the sounds of their distress had synthesised into one unearthly wail.

As midnight passed and the night of the first day of July turned towards the dawn of the second, as the gunfire died down, it seemed to fill the air. All along the front, from the orchards of Gommecourt to the heights of Beaumont Hamel, from the shoulders of Thiepval to the valley beyond La Boiselle, it rose from the battlefield into the night like the keening of a thousand banshees.

Holding grimly to the remnants of their battered trenches, the battered remnants of the Army shivered as they listened.

The Stretcher Bearers, First Aid Posts, Casualty Clearing Stations and Hospitals of the Western Front had to deal with the appalling casualties that resulted from this butchery of machine gun bullets, grenades, shrapnel, high explosives, gas, mortar, flame throwers, bayonets, clubs, bare hands and teeth. Soldiers at Verdun, possibly the most dreadful slaughter of the war, referred to the battleground there as "the mincer", and bleated like lambs on their way up the line. With similar conditions in mind, Ernst Jünger called his account of his time in the trenches *The Storm of Steel*. In various roles throughout the war, Robert Greig knew exactly the terrible nature of the injuries sustained in this carnage, but had to quickly overcome a natural horror at the sight of them as a stretcher bearer in an Aid Post:

> This was the first occasion on which I had been in an Aid Post, and though I had been a stretcher-bearer and carried many wounded, I had never really examined a badly wounded man in the light. I became physically sick as I looked at him and could feel the sweat start from my forehead. The Medical Officer also saw how I was affected, and, having drastic methods of curing the softer feelings, forthwith picked me out to assist him to dress this patient.

In the face of such destruction and terror, it was easy to lose hope, and consequently, faith. Greig makes a point of great significance about the church, that the "drum head" church parades behind the lines failed to answer the spiritual needs of many soldiers. He saw it as a wasted opportunity to bring the church and the young men of the country closer together. He felt strongly that the demands on fighting soldiers for polished buttons and the like at a service only served to create a disillusionment which would undermine the importance of the organised Christian religion in Britain. Arguably, he has been proved correct. There was a hardened sense of fatalism that existed in the trenches instead, both within a Christian framework and without. Malcolm Brown:

> For many, perhaps the majority, conventional religion could not resolve problems ... to their satisfaction, and there grew up a widespread, simply expressed fatalism, of which the essential belief was that if you were to live you were to live, if you were to die you were to die. In other words, if somewhere there was a bullet or a shell with your number on it, there was nothing you could do about it; till then just soldier on.

There is a tremendous anger simmering away in Greig's narrative, and occasionally a Lewis gun up the behind for those who try to claim the suffering of the ordinary soldier for their own agenda. In common with Sassoon and Shetland's John Peterson, Greig was already in 1920 nurturing a fury for those who publicly memorialised the gallant dead, while ignoring the needs of the gallant living. Even worse, publicly memorialising the gallant dead, but failing to admit to the great wrong of their sacrifice in the first place—a target in Peterson's "such sculpture rare" in his poem 'The Monument' and Sassoon's "sepulchre of crime"[12]. In places, Greig really lets go too:

---

12 From 'On Passing the New Menin Gate' by Siegfried Sassoon:
"Well might the dead who struggled in the slime
Rise and deride this sepulchre of crime."

And there is only one way to prevent war in the future and that is to teach in our schools and in our homes, not the honour and glory—there is very little in it—but the horror and filth of war, not to dwell on the prowess of England (it is usually England, and not Britain) as a world conqueror, but to tell the historical truth, that greed and the desire for gain have usually been the motive power behind all great wars.

Now, Greig's passionate conviction that a handful of fat-cats had grown rich on the suffering of the men in the trenches is far from an unusual attitude among ex-soldiers, but there is a real vehemence to his stance. Although not a Socialist, statements like "It was not to enable a section of the community to exploit the rest that these men fought" are reminiscent of the writing of none other than that legendary opponent of conscription, John Maclean[13]:

> We have repeatedly expressed our perfect willingness to let those who benefit by capitalism enter the war, and slaughter one another to their heart's content. That is their affair, not ours. Their mutual extermination might, in fact, smooth the path leading to socialism, so that even many socialists might be excused if they departed from the policy of indifference and became active recruiting agents amongst the propertied class, urging them with fiery eloquence to defend *their* king and *their* country.

Surviving the war, paradoxically, brought a kind of death. One of the truly great poems of the First World War is Siegfried Sassoon's 'Sick Leave'. A soldier in hospital, most likely Sassoon himself, is haunted by dreams of his comrades back in the trenches. The guilt at deserting them, allowing them to die while he still lives, is the key emotion. Implicit in the writing of Robert Greig, of his "true friend in death" for example, there is a similar sadness and guilt in having survived, while leaving some of the lads "over there". In countless memoirs, published or unpublished, this is again a common thread. Crudely put, it appears to be a psychological flip side to the relief of personal survival. The crucial factor seems to be that the intensity of the experience of the war and the intensity of friendships made under such circumstances were wound so tightly together that the worst pain was leaving a pal behind. In *Blighty: British Society in the Era of the Great War* Degroot puts it succinctly:

> Many of those who escaped death or serious injury were haunted with guilt at being singled out to survive. Death had been bizarre, mysterious, inexplicable; to go on living seemed a capricious injustice.

In 'Sick Leave', Sassoon is equally forceful:

---

[13] Trevor Royle: "As an opponent of conscription and a supporter of industrial unrest, Maclean was arrested in 1916 and sentenced to three years' penal servitude in Perth and Peterhead prisons. Released in 1917 he was re-arrested the following year and spent three further periods in prison before his final release in October 1922. Maclean's position as a socialist nationalist is unrivalled in Scottish political history..."

Out of the gloom they gather about my bed.
They whisper to my heart; their thoughts are mine.
"Why are you here with all your watches ended?
From Ypres to Frise we sought you in the Line."
In bitter safety I awake, unfriended;
And while the dawn begins with slashing rain
I think of the battalion in the mud.
"When are you going out to them again?
Are they not still your brothers through our blood?"[14]

* * * * *

After the war Robert Greig returned to work at *The Shetland Times*, eventually becoming a partner in the business, and over the years he grew to be a well liked, weel-kent member of the community. He forged ahead as a reporter with ferocious determination and conspicuous integrity, giving everything to his job, and often working full days without sleep. Like many of the Great War soldiers, the night was a difficult time. On occasion his young son Joe would see him at the typewriter at night when he went to bed and find him still there in the morning when he got up, clattering furiously at the keys, the room filled with black tobacco smoke, like 221b Baker Street locked in the grip of a three-pipe problem.

The nature of his work brought Greig into contact with folk all over Shetland: at agricultural shows, sales of work, council meetings, sports events and social functions. He met bakers, councillors, fishermen, teachers, ministers, crofters, nurses, visitors to the islands (famed or otherwise), and just about everybody else as well. People knew him for his interest in Shetland and its people, for his sense of humour, for his kindness.

When Robert Greig died suddenly in 1938 there was widespread shock and sadness. In both local papers there were tributes from those who had known him, from the organisations whose meetings he had attended for so many years. On the day of his funeral the flags at the County Buildings, The Town Hall and Fort Charlotte were flown at half mast. Bob Inkster, his long time reporting counterpart at *The Shetland News*, wrote a personal tribute[15]:

---

[14] In her novel *Regeneration*, Pat Barker imagines the real life meeting between Sassoon, patient, and W.H.R. Rivers, Army Psychologist, at Craiglockhart Army Hospital in Edinburgh. Sassoon was sent there after he was declared shell shocked by Medical Board following his public protest against the war in July 1917. In the novel, Sassoon gives Rivers 'Sick Leave' to read:

Sassoon, who'd got up and walked across to the window, turned round when a movement from Rivers seemed to indicate he'd finished. "It's all right," he said. "Don't feel you have to say something."

But Rivers was not capable of saying anything. He'd taken off his glasses and was dabbing the skin round his eyes. Sassoon didn't know what to do. He pretended to look out the window again. At last Rivers put his glasses on again and said,

"Does the question have an answer?"

"Oh, yes. I'm going back."

[15] *The Shetland News*, 31st March, 1938.

Good-natured, kindly and obliging, always unruffled and constantly showing a splendid camaraderie, you helped to lighten and brighten the daily and nightly routine of reporting. Nearly 20 years of contemporary work together brought us into close and intimate contact, and that long and happy association developed into a genuine friendship, even into affectionate regard.

And now, long before your journalistic life's work should have been completed, you have written "End of Message". The eager notebook is closed forever.

Had he lived to see the start of the Second War the following year Robert Greig would not have been surprised by Britain's return to arms; he was an astute man, and he had read the signs long before. Even as a member of the Army of Occupation in Germany he could see clearly the messy, shambolic nature of the so-called victory. In the horrible death of a young British soldier in the woods of Germany, Greig finds a bitter symbolism for this failure to tie up desperate loose ends. He knew even before he left Germany in 1919 that the great Twentieth Century world conflict was not over, merely waiting to begin again. All this he surely predicted, but he would have been appalled to discover that even now we have yet to act on the hardest learned lessons of all:

For the first great necessity to the tortured world is peace, and it is a peace that the man who knows war wants to see. Peace is a national matter, but more than that it is international. A League of Nations is a beautiful idea, and one that should at least have a fair trial; but its weakness lies in the fact that there can be no guarantee that the nations comprising the League may not themselves quarrel. A democratic Army, where every man is a soldier, may be a good idea, but its weakness is that such an army is apt to breed militarism, while it naturally follows that the country or Empire with the greatest number of men and the greatest wealth, becomes a menace to the rest of the world. The only real solution is the total disarmament of the world, the disbanding of every fighting unit, and the conversion of factories for the manufacture of weapons of war into workshops for the manufacture of the tools of peace. The glamour of war must be killed and the children of the world taught that there is no glamour, only torture and grief, only death and desolation. But these things must be international and world wide, though there is no reason why our school books with their savage glorying in the bloodshed of the past should not now be scrapped and rewritten in such a spirit that the children learning from them might grow up determined that there shall be no more war. That would be a step in the right direction, and with the coming of a world peace there should also come a world prosperity.

Doing His Bit is no wail from a malcontent. It is the simple truth, as a soldier sees it.

Alex Cluness,
January, 1999.

I
THE EDGES OF THINGS
10TH JANUARY, 1920

I HEARD A story some time ago of a gentleman who, anxious to know the real facts about the war, ordered through an agency all the authentic histories of the gigantic struggle through which Europe has recently passed. Hardly had the armistice been signed than the first of these arrived, and they continued to arrive at such pace that the gentleman had to make his house his library and build himself an outhouse as a dwelling-place, this, in due course, becoming an overflow for the library. And so I wish to make it clear that the articles which appear under this heading are not a history; they are merely the edges of things as seen by the man in the ranks, the actual experiences of a "Tommy", or more accurately a "Jock", to whom the joys and the sorrows of the campaign came, not as something purely personal, but as the common lot of the millions of citizen soldiers who offered and were often individually asked to surrender their all that Britain might be free, that Right should triumph over Wrong, and that peace might be bought, at no matter what cost, for a suffering world.

These experiences are necessarily limited to the immediate environment of the soldier concerned, and cannot possibly represent what actually took place in any wide area, for it must be understood that, while one might hear of the results of any operation after it was over, it was impossible to take more than even a passing interest in one's nearest neighbours; and that only, not because one felt any special concern as to the safety or otherwise of these neighbours, but because it was necessary to "feel" these men, and also because it kept one from feeling any oppressive loneliness in times of stress.

The average soldier is a very inarticulate mortal. He suffers, and he buries his suffering under a bushel of silence, admitting only that this was "pretty rotten," or that was "pretty hot while it lasted." But he has suffered and the suffering has left its mark. The bitter experiences picked up in the battle areas, which have left our youths men and our young men old beyond their years, where ages were lived in an hour and undreamed terrors were faced and overcome—these experiences cannot be eradicated in a year, not in a lifetime. And it is as a mouthpiece of these men that I take up my pen in an endeavour to put before those who do not know—and no-one can conceive of war who has not had the actual experience—some of those happenings which made up the daily life of those who fought that others might not know what fighting meant.

I know, of course, that it is a long time since the cessation of hostilities, a mass of matter written in regard to the war; but I do not think that there has been any attempt to set down the life as lived by the private soldier, who was to the officer a unit, a pawn in the game, a cog in the great machine. As such, he was not supposed to have a mind with which to think, nor intelligence with which to grasp the meaning of a simple sentence; but it was in him all the time that the nation trusted, and did not trust in vain. The "unit" was a giant of endurance and a slave only to duty, and it is this man's point of view that I am going to try, as far as I am capable, to put before those who may find this column of interest.

Perhaps I should explain here that, though I kept a diary from the time I crossed over to France, I had the misfortune to lose it, together with some much more important kit, at the time of the German advance in March[1], since which time I made no attempt to keep a personal record of the incidents which occurred in the Battalion to which I was posted. Wherefore I do not propose to write these articles in anything like a chronological order, I shall endeavour, however, to keep things in "sections," as it were, so that we may march forward from Shetland to peace—and after—as smoothly as possible.

There is only one aim in these notes, and that is to set before you the soldier, and not the man or the boy as he was before he was a soldier, not the man as he appears to be to-day, but the man you never saw and never knew, who lived like an animal and died like an angel; and to point out that no one can afford to judge him or condemn him, and that every-one—including his fellow-soldiers—owes him a debt which cannot really be repaid. I have seen in Aberdeen, and Lerwick, too, ex-soldiers, anxious and willing to work, but finding no employment; and I say, without fear of contradiction from any right-thinking person, that those things should not be. The men ask only the right to earn, and that surely should not be denied them, for if they have not won the freedom to live, who, indeed, has earned that modest privilege?

I should like to ask the readers of these notes, in concluding this introductory article, to remember that Britain, which so many people—and particularly Britishers—delight in belittling, did far more actually to win this war than did any other nation engaged—that she spent more, "enthused" more, and gave more than either France or Belgium, and that she raised, to the astonishment of the world, and to the lasting grief of Germany, an impossible Army from peace-loving and peace-thinking citizens, who, in splendid spirit added glory and honour to the already golden archives of the British Army, than which there is no finer and no more chivalrous on the face of the earth. Well can one who has fought with these soldiers and lived among them sympathise with Germany in the stricken agony which produced her famous—or is notorious the word?—hymns of hate and her devout prayer—"Gott strafe England!"

I do not wish to dwell at any great length on the soldier's life on this side of the Channel, but I should like to give my impression of the difficulties of the Shetlander who has to join up in the south. He has thrust upon him with great force in a case of that kind the insularity of Shetland and its limitations as a centre of the universe. I left Lerwick in the summer, and had as good a run

---

[1]   The German advance Greig refers to, Operation Michael, began at 9.30 a.m. on the 21st March, 1918. The Germans called it "Kaiserschlacht" – The Kaiser's Battle. Martin Middlebrook's *The Kaiser's Battle* is an excellent account.

south as one can expect over the particular piece of water which crossing to Aberdeen involves, and arrived there in time to catch a train for Fort George, where I had to report. I do not know how many of the readers of this journal have travelled by the Highland Railway. Those who have not should not.

In due course I arrived at Fort George—a very dismal place, right on the seashore—and entered barracks, which looked to me exactly like a prison. I should not have been surprised to see the "Abandon hope" inscription over the door, and I certainly felt very small and forlorn, and not at all military-like, as I passed the man on gate duty, who curtly directed me to the orderly room where I handed in my papers to a cheerful clerk, who told me that I would not have to stay there, for which, he remarked, I should be very thankful. I was devoutly so. I was then directed to a place to get breakfast, and told to be about the Orderly Room when the doctor came in. As I did not know when the doctor would come in I did not go to breakfast, but strolled over to the Post Office— which is inside the barracks—and sent off a telegram to inform the folks at home of my safe arrival on the mainland. I was strolling leisurely across the square when I heard my name shouted and saw an excited individual, wearing tartan trousers, and holding a sheaf of papers in his hand, running about the door of the Orderly Room. I casually walked across and asked him if he wanted me. He looked at me sternly and told me in no measured terms, that I was a soldier now and had better "double to it—the M.O. was waiting."

I saw the doctor, who handed my papers to a clerk, who asked me to wait a moment. I stood about for some half-hour and then the messenger appeared again, thrust my papers into my hand, and said briefly and with unnecessary cheerfulness—"You're for Sheffield." He then left me.

Having no idea as to when a train left for the south, I could only take up my meagre bundle and go to the station. As I passed the gate duty man he asked me where I was for. "Sheffield," I said. "You lucky devil," was his only comment as he recommenced to pace up and down. I reached the station, having had no food for about a couple of days—not being the best of sailors— I did not risk a meal on board the steamer—and had to wait some considerable time for a train. Then the Highland Railway again to Inverness. I travelled all that day, and late at night I arrived at York. Cold, hungry and lonely, I had to wait there until seven o'clock next morning. I tried to get a cup of tea and something to eat at a sailors' and soldiers' buffet, but I was unsuccessful as I did not have on a uniform. I explained that I was going to have one, and even produced my papers to prove it. The lady in charge expressed her sorrow, but was adamant. At six o' clock however, the railway buffet opened, and I had my first meal for some three days—two cups of tea and some railway sandwiches. I landed in Sheffield bright and early, went to a barber shop and had a shave and wash up so that I might be presentable when I appeared at wherever I had to go. I tried a few soldiers to see if they knew my destination, but they could not direct me. Finally, I approached a policeman, and he handed me over to a military policeman, who put me on a tramcar which landed me at the barrack gate.

The picquet at the gate passed me into the Guard Room, where a sergeant pounced at me, took me to a table, and produced some books. Politely I took off my cap on entering the Guard Room, but the sergeant shouted with great fervour—"Keep your cap on here!" so I meekly resumed it. He then took some particulars about me and sent a man across to a barrack room with me. I was then very hungry, so I asked him about something to eat. My guide was very brief—"Dinner up at 12.45," he said. He showed me into a large, airy, bare-walled, cold-looking, unhomelike room, in which was collected some half-dozen civilians looking very glum. As I entered, a lance-corporal with several good conduct chevrons told one of the men to show me how to make a bed. The bed was a small iron bedstead in two parts, one of which pushed under the other, making a seat; there were three "biscuits," hard, solid-like mattresses; three blankets, and a little round pillow stuffed hard with straw.

The bed made up to the satisfaction of the lance-corporal, he briskly unmade it and told me to try myself. I did so with sufficient success to please him. As it was still some time till dinner appeared, he set us on to dry scrub the floor of the room, and impressed us with the necessity of cleanliness, and particularly his desire that we should keep this room spotless. I was by this time quite anxious about my dinner, and when it came I hurried outside—we had our meals outside under a veranda in summer—to the tables. Two of the men were sent for a "dixie" of stew, and this they dished out in large plates. The stew was very floppy and fatty, and this, together with the fact that I felt very lonely and hardly dealt with in having to sojourn in such a prison-like home, did not add zest to the meal, from which I arose as hungry as when I sat down.

Later in the day other men came into the room, and soon we were "A full house." We all went to bed early, as we had nothing else to do, and almost all night, I lay awake tossing on the hard mattress, and vainly trying to keep warm under what was to me an inadequate covering, Later, I would have considered these amenities to life the acme of luxury, but I had a great deal to learn. And so ended my first day in barracks.

II
MEN AND YET MORE MEN
17TH JANUARY, 1920

I DO NOT intend to dwell at any great length on the life of the soldier on this side of the Channel, but there are one or two phases of that life which might prove of interest to those who did not have an opportunity of serving with the colours. In the first place a consideration of barrack life should not come amiss. The civilian enters the barracks a social unit, a man who has had to face difficulties, who has had to use initiative, and map out to a large extent his own life. Shortly after his arrival in barracks he dons khaki, and thereupon becomes one of a number of men, all equal, with someone above him to straighten out his difficulties, without the opportunity, indeed with practically an order not to use initiative and with his life practically from day to day mapped out for him. Instead of an operation requiring the use of his limbs and his brain, he is paraded and inspected, and drilled until he can do what is expected mechanically. That he might not have an opportunity to think, he has to keep a set of equipment in a high state of polish, keep his buttons bright, keep his barrack room clean and tidy, and in addition has to do scullion work in the cookhouse, the sergeants' mess, and the officers' mess, all of which tends to lower the mental calibre and bring the man to an actual lower state of civilisation than that when he entered the Army. This retrograde process certainly makes splendid soldiers, but it makes poor civilians, and yet we have people who do not know what the training really was, and who only saw the physical effect—which was generally an improvement—making derogatory remarks about the men on whom the training left those results which were inevitable from its methods. These people who, knowing nothing of even the training for war, much less of war itself, were loudest in their cries of "carry on," and glibbest in their eulogies of the citizen army, should have been ready with a constructive policy in order that the victims of their patriotism should have been received in "a country fit for heroes to live in," and not in a country which cannot offer profitable employment to the men who are left, even though some million, previously employed, laid down their lives.

Personally, I did not find barrack life so very hard after I had got into the routine, but I was fortunate in that the N.C.O.'s we had were good fellows, we did not have too many officers, and the food was neither bad nor insufficient. I know, however, that in several camps food was often insufficient and badly cooked, in others the N.C.O.s gave men a rough time, and the more inoffensive the soldier, the rougher the time he had, while in other camps, where there were more officers than jobs to go round, the life of the soldier was made a thorny one by their meddling.

Camp life was, naturally, a great deal worse than barrack life. Camps were usually built away from towns of any great size, and were generally crowded with troops, so that a man had few opportunities of amusement or distraction other than in the company of his fellow-soldiers, and their horizon was generally bounded by the camp, home, France, and their best girls. In fine weather, living under canvas, after the novelty wore off, was not quite so pleasant as it might be. For one thing, the tents were generally over-crowded, so that it was very difficult to get sleeping room. Then to add to the general discomfort, it was impossible to leave any of it outside, so that kit-bags, packs, etc., had also to be stored in these tents. Added to all these inconveniences the warmth seemed to attract all crawling things, especially earwigs, which kept one lively when one would have slept.

In wet weather a camp was pretty horrible. The paths throughout soon became ankle-deep in mud, and at night the "floor" of the tent, the earth, was damp, and often itself a few inches deep in mud, from which the waterproof sheet one slept on was quite inadequate to protect the would-be sleeper. At night too, one had always to be watchful, in case a guy snapped, or the tent-pole broke or the tent came down, or was blown away. All of which did not tend to allow one the balm of a good night's rest. Then, when the rain cleared off, a great moment of cleaning up fell to the lot of the hopeless soldier whose drills, of course, could not be curtailed when the cry was for "men and yet more men."

The ideal life was life in billets. I had the great good fortune to spend a winter billeted up on civilians in a town in the north of England. There I had a feather bed, all that man could desire for food, and a warm fire every night, besides the company of civilians with other interests than mere soldiering, and therefore conversation that took one away from all the pettiness that was one's life! It was a glorious change, and one that ended all too soon. While I was in this billet the old gentleman of the house died, and I had a day off to go to his funeral. He was a Catholic and the funeral was a magnificent and impressive one, but what was my astonishment on returning to the billet to find that the occasion had been made the opportunity for a feast, and I sat down to a spread that would have gladdened the eyes of all the troops in the Regiment.

I subsequently left this billet for another, where I spent my first Christmas in khaki. Here the people looked after us like sons, and on Christmas day gave us such a dinner as one does not expect outside of home. Certainly the billet in "Blighty" is the best place in which to do one's soldiering.

After training, I spent some time in barracks, camps, and billets, I was sent to huts. There life could be very uncomfortable, as more often than not the huts were not wind proof, and, as in the case of a camp, the ground became a quagmire in times of rain. However, as I always had a sufficiency of food and clothing, I was not dissatisfied with the life in Britain, though it certainly did not do much to broaden one's outlook or improve one morally or mentally.

I was for a brief period on the office staff of the unit to which I was posted, but soon gave up the work. The work to which I was set could have been rapidly carried out by a boy of fourteen and I felt that to a man willing and healthy enough to do some real work to bring victory nearer, such employment was nothing short of an insult. Had I known, however, what was meant by "real work" I think I would have accepted the "insult" smiling.

Perhaps I can best conclude this article with a sketch of a draft leaving for the front. I saw three leave before I left myself, and each time, in my ignorance, I was consumed with a vast jealousy for each individual member of the drafts. The first I saw was for the East. With their pith helmets and khaki drill they looked a very fine body of men, and fully two-thirds of them had been drinking the healths of their friends prior to leaving, with the result that the Regimental Sergeant-Major had his work cut out to keep them in line. They literally staggered off to the strains of the band, and vanished into the station, and I never saw any of them again. The other two drafts went off late at night, but they went sober, not from any desire to be so on their part, but because they had been in camps throughout the day, and so had had no opportunities to be festive. At last the day came when I too was put on draft, also for the East. At last I was satisfied. I enjoyed my full days of kit-inspections, of drawing one kit and handing in another, of inspections and medical inspections and general inspections and waited expectantly until the day came when, in the evening, we were to move off, and take the initial step in "the Great Adventure."

III
A VERY TERRIBLE JOURNEY
7TH FEBRUARY, 1920

I DO NOT know if the experience I propose to narrate has been the common lot of the soldier, though some undoubtedly have endured it, but it should prove of interest to Shetland readers as it has certainly fallen to the lot of countless of her sons. This was really my first "adventure," and it opened my eyes that "war was not all it was cracked up to be" by the speakers and writers on the subject. This narrative is necessarily egoistic, but I hope my readers will excuse that on this occasion, as under the circumstances, I could not possibly write from the point of view of anyone but myself.

After being satiated with all sorts of inspections, after being paraded and re-paraded, after being told to hold ourselves in readiness to leave "within a couple of days," perhaps half a dozen times, we, a small draft for the East, were at last astounded to hear that we were actually going! We were delighted to get away. Like all soldiers we found a thousand good reasons to "grouse" at everything about the camp we were leaving, and we painted the East a glorious red and gold, a land of milk and honey much to be desired before the barren wilderness of a camp in "Blighty." Our jubilant spirits continued with us when we marched to the station, headed by the band, and cheered by the poor unfortunates who were left to the drudgery of a peaceful training at home! But most of us felt depressed when we got shoved into our various compartments, and knew that we were actually leaving home for no one knew how long. Not that we showed our depression. Rather there was a suspicious increase in our hilarity which reached its climax as the train steamed out to the strains of "Auld Lang Syne" and the concentrated roar of the boys we were leaving behind. I don't think many of us, as the train proceeded, felt the size of our hats so large as when we marched up the quiet, dark streets from the camp to the station, shouting our "good-byes" to the good times we had had as the sure conquerors of Germany.

Our spirits were further damped by the journey to Le Havre—at least, that was the case with some of us, for we had a pretty rough crossing, and not many of us were cut out as navy men. We spent a night at Le Havre and entrained, with other drafts, for a journey across France to Marseilles. All this sounds very interesting and instructive. We thought so, too, but as we proceeded on our journey we changed our minds. It was very interesting at first, but it soon became only tiresome and finally bored one to tears almost. The journey occupied between seven and eight days, and we travelled in trucks, not carriages. These, of course, have no windows, only a sliding door on each side. They were uncomfortably filled, and travelled at the convenience of all the other traffic on the line. It was, on the whole, a very terrible journey, and only our capacity for sleep made it endurable. It was at night when we arrived at Marseilles, and we went, it appeared to us, out of the town to a small village where we embarked. We were very weary after our journey, and we were exceedingly glad to see the vessel on which we were to take the longer journey. We hurried to our quarters—and when I say "hurried" I use it in the military sense, which meant being hung up every here and there for at least half an hour—and I was, fortunately for me I thought, one of the first to get on board the steamer. Our quarters were aft, and I got a lower hammock. I may mention that the transports to the East were pretty well gutted out, and then hammocks were swung from the floor to the roof (if floor and roof are the maritime terms for what I mean). My pal had the hammock above me, and, after sentries were set, we were very glad to "turn to" and have a sleep on a bed that was comparatively stationary. Of course when he had got into bed we had all the usual jokes about mal de mer and torpedoes passed around till conversation gradually languished and we slept. Some of the men were wakened as the transport got under way, but they soon drowsed off again, and the only sounds that disturbed the night were the lap of the water against the sides of the vessel, the rhythmical throb of the engines, and the two-hourly impatient calls from the sentries for their reliefs and the protesting grunts of the newly-awakened soldiers unwilling to take up their duties.

I was very suddenly and rudely awakened by a terrific crash. I knew right away what had happened, and before I was properly awake I was on the floor of our "berth" and getting into some clothes. I saw the rush for the stairs as I dressed, and then I, too, hurried out on deck with my life-belt—for each man had been provided with one as he entered the ship—in my hand. I discovered that I had made two mistakes. First, I shouldn't have dressed, and, second, I should have put on my life-belt. It is quite as cold in the water with all one's clothes on as without them, and to carry a life-belt meant, in my case, to lose it.

When I got on deck the steamer was going down by the bows and the stern was high in the air. Several people were shouting, and some stertorian voice was advising everybody in general that it was "everyone for himself." So I went to the rail and lingered there awhile, loth to leave the solidity of the deck for the tender mercies of the ocean. However, I finally jumped overboard, and it felt a terrible drop. Naturally, I went under, and when I came to the surface, spluttering, I discovered that I had dropped my life-belt. I expect, but I am not very sure, that I dropped it in stretching out my hands to save myself from receiving any hurt as I hit the water. I am not a swimmer, but I struck out, and I had hardly started, when I struck my knuckles on a piece of wood. It was a good piece of wood, just about the right size for me, being about the length of my arms, and giving a grip at the other side. I took a good hold and then waited.

While I waited, I discovered several things. I found out that the water was quite cold. I also found out that the little waves—it was almost calm—had a nasty habit of slapping one's face quite hard. I saw, too, several chaps floating about, and one or two swimming, and I heard several crying out. I then discovered a very awkward thing. The engines had been left running, with the result that the propeller was tearing round, for the stern of the vessel had lifted high by this time. The "draw" of the propeller was pulling the men near to it, with the result that a great many were injured and some were killed, among the latter being my pal who had his head smashed. I do not know how I escaped injury, but I think the propeller was clear of the water when I passed under it, for I heard it "snore" and think—though I possibly imagined it—that I felt the wind from it. Fortunately, I was swept well clear of the vessel then, which shortly afterwards dived down, though I did not see her go, but I distinctly felt the "pull" of the water.

For some little time I had some difficulty to keep my piece of wood. Several men tried to take it from me, but they had life-belts and I had none, so I fought for it. I had rather a shock at that time, as someone came up at my back and pushed me. I freed one hand and pushed him away. He came again and I repeated the performance, but I was very weary and did not feel very fit to struggle much longer. He came again, however, and, exasperated, I pulled him round to have a look at such a determined attacker, for one hard push had satisfied the other claimants to my board. When I got him heaved round I was very shocked to see that he was quite dead and floating on his life-belt. I was actually physically sick at the sight of it.

I floated about for some time—it looked to me like years—and became colder and colder and more hopeless. I even tried to let go my board, but my hands refused to slip, and I clung on. At length I was picked up by a French destroyer, and taken on board. I did not know the destroyer was there and was not at all excited. However, after I had been stripped, rubbed down, and warmly rolled up, had a drink of coffee "with something in it," and a cigarette—a horrible French one—between my lips, I cheered up considerably and soon slept soundly. We were put ashore at Marseilles, and into a hospital there, but we did not stay long—that is, those of us who were uninjured and not suffering from shock. We were sent back to "Blighty," and even returned to the company which we left. I turned up clad in a pair of khaki trousers, a blue jacket on the sleeves of which was much red braid, a pair of red slippers, and my own cap! My cap and badge were all I had saved from the wreck. Needless to say we were the heroes for a day or two, but soon we were down to the old routine, and very soon our first adventure felt a long way off.

While we were at Marseilles I saw a great many convalescent camps, and spoke to a number of men who had been "up the line" in France. They, after my recent experience, did much to dull the edge of my enthusiasm to "see things," as they actually were in France and Flanders. All had a similar tale to tell of filth and horror, without any good thing to say of war, and nearly all solemnly assured me that they meant to "swing it" in the south of France to the limit of their ingenuity. However, that sort of talk did not impress one to the extent that was necessary to bring before one the real terrors of war, and to determine one that wars must cease for all time, and that never more should men have to live and suffer—and die—under such conditions of dirt and distress as prevailed throughout this war. And there is only one way to prevent war in the future, and that is to teach in our schools and in our homes, not the honour and glory—there is very little in it—but the horror and filth of war, not to dwell on the prowess of England (it is usually England, and not Britain) as a world conqueror, but to tell the historical truth, that greed and the desire for gain have usually been the motive power behind all great wars.

IV
WAS THAT NOT TOO LONG?
14TH FEBRUARY, 1920

WHEN I GOT back to Britain, after my initiatory experience of the "real thing," I was fortunate in having some more training before again being sent abroad. I did not wish to dwell on the home training, but things which seem to me of interest keep recurring to my mind, and I feel that it would be better to write them down and give my readers common enough happenings but giving them from the soldiers' point of view. And so, when I mean to take those who may find this column perusable across to France with me on the first stage of the journey which meant so much, not only to those who took it, but to civilisation, I find my thoughts wandering from France to the delights of leave, and to one or two experiences I had in camps in Britain.

Leave meant a very great deal to the soldier. For one thing it meant a visit to the family circle, with all its attendant variety, after some dreary months of monotonous training, with its monotonous colour scheme, its monotonous menu, its monotonous barracks or hutments or tents, and its monotonous obedience to what appeared to most men ridiculous orders. And my personal opinion, for what it is worth, is that that very monotony was really responsible for the vast majority of war marriages, for to men who were continually among men and at the mercy of the harpies of the streets, practically the only women with whom so far as my experience went, the private soldier, in a strange place had an opportunity to associate, the sight of an honest woman, known to the soldier, and respected by him, was almost sufficient to make him take the plunge into the matrimonial sea. Leave, besides its relaxation from monotony, also meant a bed. To those who have not had to suffer the discomfort of an Army bed, with the drab blankets, the yearning of the soldier for something soft to be on, and something that could look clean, must ever remain a mystery. Not that the home bed when one got to it, was really satisfactory—it was generally found too soft and too warm to allow of the lover of comfort getting any sleep, and he was fain to turn out with a couple of blankets on the floor that he might have rest, only he didn't like, not knowing how the people at home might take his little peculiarities.

Personally, as in the case of everything connected with the Army, I was particularly fortunate in my leaves, but I should like to say a word about those unfortunate Shetlanders who were not. A very great number of them, when they got their draft leave, reached Aberdeen, only to discover that no boat would leave until it made a visit home impossible. I have been told by one or two of these lads of their visiting the steamers at the quay at Aberdeen just to talk to someone who had seen Lerwick recently and could give them a little verbal news, so much more acceptable, than even long accounts of local happenings, in the "home letter" or *The Shetland Times*. On the first occasion I got leave I "wangled" through the good offices of my Company Sergeant-Major and an Orderly Room Staff-Sergeant fourteen days, instead of the usual seven, my own imaginative word pictures of the isolation of the Shetland Islands and the difficulties of access thereto aiding me materially in having my request granted. I left the town in which I was billeted in the north of England about 8 p.m. one evening, and right through I seemed to be unable to go wrong. At each place where a change was necessary there was a train ready to start, and I reached Aberdeen just half an hour before the boat left direct for Scalloway, so that I landed in Lerwick, having been driven there from Scalloway in a Naval car, within a little more than 24 hours of my leaving my billet. This must seem incredible, and does even to me yet, but it actually happened, though I never heard of any other soldier on leave being quite so fortunate. The unfortunate thing was that, as I had got 14 days, I did not want to overstay my furlough, and so had to leave home some days prior to its expiry, and things of less moment have caused much swearing among "the troops."

On the second occasion on which I got leave I got just seven days. The Orderly Room had apparently discovered Shetland! I reached Aberdeen and waited two days on a boat, and then took over one day to reach Lerwick. I then discovered that, to get back in time, I would have to leave the same night (or perhaps early next morning), which of course, was impossible. So I waited till another boat left Lerwick. During the time I waited a boat left Scalloway, but the O.C. troops in Shetland blinked this fact with the result that, when I returned to camp some five days overdue, and when I presented the explanatory note from the O.C. troops the Company Officer did not think it worth while making a case of it; so, as I said, good luck dogged my steps in this, as in all else, during my service with H.M. forces. Other men, however, were not so fortunate, and those Shetlanders who did manage to reach home had a very brief respite from the "dreary round" till they had to undertake what is surely the most wearisome of journeys back again, and especially wearisome to those to whom the sea is, as it is to me, anathema.

I mentioned that I felt the desire to tell of one or two incidents that befell me in camp before I "went foreign," and these subjects, not very cheerful reading, are about two cases of suicide with which I was personally connected. In both instances I blamed (this is again my personal opinion) not the training nor the Army, but the Medical Boards who passed the men for service, and the Tribunals which sent the men to serve. In both cases I should imagine that the Tribunals must have known the circumstances of the men; but in any case it is inconceivable that these circumstances were not put before these Tribunals when appeal was being made that the men should not be called up. Both men were mentally defective, and, like all unbalanced people, showed great astuteness in the carrying out of their designs.

The first case was that of a man who was obviously "not all there." We were under canvas at the time, and this recruit, not even receiving a suit of khaki, was put in a tent apart from the others and two men were detailed to observe him, a full guard being mounted at night in order that two men might be beside him at night also! It was lovely weather at the time, and one Sunday I was selected as an observer together with another man who had seen active service. We lazed about in the sun on the grass and took an occasional peep at the recumbent figure in the tent, who was to all appearances sleeping the day away. I arranged with my co-observer to go for dinner first, so that he was left alone in charge, and I went. After about three-quarters of an hour's absence I returned, and was somewhat taken aback to see quite a crowd near the tent, and the Transport Officer, a splendid specimen, before the door. As I came nearer the latter strode up and inquired vociferously as to who I was and what I wanted there. I explained mildly that I was one of the observers. He then asked me where I had been, with accompanying epithets. I again mildly explained that I had been to dinner. How long had I been away? About three-quarters of an hour. Was that not too long? No, I didn't think so; the men were allowed an hour and a half, and in civil life were allowed an hour. Well, it was quite long enough for——to have hanged himself. I was to consider myself under open arrest for neglect of duty, etc.; and my heart sank and I was sore afraid. The recruit had hanged himself from the tent pole with a thin leather strap he used in lieu of braces, and had been hanging so low that he had to bend his knees to keep his feet from the ground. He must have seized a moment when my co-observer's attention was attracted elsewhere, and he must have been most cautious in his movements and determined in his aim.

In due course the civil police arrived, and I was hailed before them and told my story. My co-observer, who was also under open arrest, was also questioned. Later there was an inquest, and the parents of the dead man were present. His mother wept throughout the whole proceedings which were very depressing, and I was really very sad at heart that day. We, the observers, were exonerated at the Court, and were later, as we were under open arrest—that is, we could not leave the camp, but otherwise "carried on"—brought before the Colonel, who gave us a fatherly lecture and dismissed us. So that, officially, as well as to my own satisfaction, I was not held in any degree responsible for the death of a man who should never have been in the Army.

The second case was just as bad, if not worse. The man was called up, and sulked in his tent—he was not under observation—for three days, refusing to do drills or eat or go out, and one bright forenoon, when the lines were practically deserted, severed his wrist with a razor. He was found bleeding freely, by a sergeant who speedily stopped the flow of blood and had him removed to hospital. I helped to carry him down, and once or twice sat by his bedside, keeping him, after this outbreak, under observation. He made slow progress, for a wrist, deeply hacked with even an Army razor, does not heal readily. However, he did improve, but always lay quiet in his bed, probably brooding, for he seldom spoke. I was not present when he finally made an end of his life; in fact, I was in France, but one of my pals with whom I kept in touch, sent me a cutting from one of the local papers giving details of his demise. It appears that in the bed next to him was a patient just undergoing an operation, and a nurse was shaving the part of his body where the incision was to be made. When she had finished she laid the razor on the edge of the bed, and our resourceful recruit, who was apparently dozing, and was under the eye of an observer, sitting between him and the man awaiting the operation, jumped up, seized the razor, and cut his throat. He was so quick and so determined about it that he practically severed his head from his body, and literally fell back on his bed a lifeless corpse.

V
A FIGHTING UNIT IN A FIGHTING MOB
28TH FEBRUARY, 1920

AFTER BEING fortunate enough to put in some training in a camp in Blighty, over and above the training necessary to make one proficient for draft, I at length was put on a draft for France. The draft consisted of about equal parts of recruits who knew nothing of war, and "old soldiers," men who had been "over there" before, and were heartily sick of war. Some of these latter were "doing time," spending their last days prior to crossing to France in the Guard Room, mostly for overstaying leave and desertion. Those men had rather a rough time, and when it was quite "on the boards" that these were their last days in the home country, their lot struck me as being particularly hard. However, one had to remember that desertions could not be allowed at a time when man-power was essential to the cause, and it was necessary to put restraint on those men who could not be trusted to "play the game;" but it nevertheless troubled me at least to see men couped up and deprived of their liberty when they were leaving Britain, perhaps for the last time. I am going to devote a little space to giving those men who do not know some idea of how they fared before leaving home for the battle front.

The prisoners on draft were not set free to do their drills and spend the last few days of their training with their pals. Those who had overstayed their leave and had short periods of time to serve were set free on the draft leaving, but up to that time they appeared on parade under escort, did their final intensive training and drew their kit under like conditions. The other prisoners, the deserters, which generally meant those, while having no intention to leave the Army without their services, had taken the opportunity to have a "fling" at home until brought to book by the military police—the deserters, having been Court Martialled and sentenced to a longer term of detention, went to France under escort. That is to say, they went to France under the direct supervision of an N.C.O., and a man, and sometimes the supervision was so close and direct that the prisoner went hand-cuffed to one of the escorts—a painful memory of a farewell to "Blighty," and not a great encouragement cheerfully to shed his life-blood for England, home and beauty. I may mention here that, owing to the fact that, on long train journeys, some of the men made a bid for liberty and the "final fling," several drafts suffered the indignity of travelling through Britain in coaches which were carefully keyed! That sort of thing did not make for the enthusiastic self-sacrifice of which I have read so often in the press; and it says much for the men that they did not bear the malice they would have been justified in bearing, but were quite willing to "carry on," while grumbling nevertheless at being treated like prisoners or, worse still, slaves. This lack of trust in the men in nearly all things was something that had to be endured to be understood. A man in France was never told where he was going, nor what he was going to do when he got there. He was told to be prepared to "move off" at such and such a time, and that was the extent of his information. To anyone with the slightest intelligence and independence this lack of trust was always irksome, and made one feel really rebellious at times. For men, who were surely doing the work of men and facing dangers which, after two thousand years of Christianity no man should have been asked to endure, to be treated like so many irresponsible school children had the effect on me, at any rate, of, to use an expressive if not very literary phrase, "getting my back up."

But to return to the prisoners. Once these men got to France, under escort, they were, with the rest of the draft, "handed over," and the prisoners were put in the Guard Room. They were later paraded before the draft to which they belonged, and probably before other soldiers also, and the charge and the finding of the Court Martial was read out and they were sent to their Unit with their draft or part of it. Here only did they get their liberty, and those who have been on active service only can appreciate what that "liberty" amounted to. Those who find this column of interest will also learn the futility of talking of liberty in connection with a man on any front in times of war.

All this, as my co-contributor "Current Topics" would say, is digression. What I really started to tell you of was the draft and its landing in France. After the draft had been formed we drew all the trench "kit," steel helmets, gas masks, etc., and handed in our spare kit, including our trousers and spare tunic, and generally felt very much like real soldiers and much less like the toy brand.

14

We had finished doing things for fun and were on our way to do things in earnest—finished with stabbing quiescent socks with bayonets, and feeling capable of going through as many Germans as came within bayonet reach, finished our rifle practice and our "swank over the top stunts", our night manoeuvres and our "digging in" practice, had tested our gas masks and gone through the gas chamber, had endured all the usual inspections, and, in fact, done everything that military genius could think of to make us good soldiers, and were still fit to "go across." And one night we left. A brass band played us away, and some of the soldiers sang as we went along. I don't know the name of the march the band played, but I do remember that the words sung to the music were—"We'd be far better off in a home." When we got to the end of our march the band played "Auld Lang Syne," and hurried back, conscious of the fact that drafts may come and drafts may go, but reveille does not change.

When we entrained, to the music of the usual cheers, we met our conducting officer. It should be understood that drafts, like parcels, were sent out in a special way, under special officers, and "handed over" like a herd of cattle at the other end. These Conducting Officers did their duty well and sometimes had a few "tough customers" to look after, which presumably accounted for the distressed and harassed appearance of the old gentleman who "conducted" us to France. He told us, as he no doubt had told every draft he had "conducted," and as he maybe believed, but which none of the draft would accept without a pinch of salt, that his only regret was that his age prevented him from going right on with us. He also held out an alluring picture of a good breakfast in London, and generally made himself agreeable; but he "kept his eye on us" and made sure at every stop that we were all there. On the whole I rather liked him and did not envy him his job. Even at the time when the troops went to France under "lock and key" he had his hands full, for in some mysterious way a door would be found open and some of the boys were not above slipping out through a window when the train stopped anywhere, to see if there "was any grub going," or merely "to stretch his legs"—he was fed up sitting still!

There was no doubt about it but that we got a good breakfast in London, and proceeded to the coast where we had dinner in a hotel taken over by the Government for the lodgement of troops awaiting embarkation abroad, and very much the worse for it! Soldiering does not enhance the domestic side of the character, and there is a regal disregard for other people's property displayed by the British "Tommy" which would break the heart of any economist. We subsequently embarked and reached Calais in about an hour and a half. The outstanding feature of that voyage to me was that I was not sea-sick! Comfort in the journey across was not one of the items on the credit side of our account with the "powers that be." The boat was packed and each man had to wear a lifebelt which, though useful, is neither ornamental nor conducive to comfort. Having landed, we were marched to the Étaples base, and there we were put under canvas—over-crowded of course—to await a further period of intensive training in the "bull-ring"—the name given to those

15

training grounds, which a soldier, having once gone over, is never likely to forget.

I saw a great deal in the press about the colossal preparations made for the reception for American troops, and the gigantic size of their base, but little was said of the perfect arrangements made for the handling of British soldiers, and little of the fact that the American preparations were only possible because of the experience gained by the British Authorities as the war progressed. The camp at Étaples was prodigious—a veritable city of huts and tents—and the ease and rapidity with which troops could be received and dispatched to any part of the British front were matters to cause wonder in the mind of anyone who gave the question the slightest consideration.

Étaples was a city founded on sand. There was sand everywhere, and the training ground was simply a desert. All drafts, in the earlier stages, had to go over this training ground and it was a heart-breaking performance. The soldiers paraded in full pack after breakfast, and with a "haversack ration" for dinner— a piece of bread or a couple of biscuits and a bit of bully beef—they were marched to the parade ground—a considerable distance—and then were bandied from pillar to post, from instructor to instructor, without rest and always hard at it, among sand and always hard at it. A man, even in good condition, did not feel bright when he returned for tea, for which the hard day in the open had given him a hearty appetite.

Subsequently there was a great riot at Étaples[2]. I do not know the true story of this riot, but it started in good earnest with the shooting by a military policeman of a Gordon N.C.O. Thereafter the Colonial troops took a hand in the game, and there was a considerable number of casualties as the result of this imbroglio. When things reached their normal state again the "bull-ring" was no more—any soldier who went through it will agree that this was worth a few dead military policemen! The most persistent rumour in regard to the commencement of the riot was that it was a case of "cherchez la femme"—a W.A.A.C. having been the cause of the first trouble. I do not know if this was the case; but, if so, though I deplore the fact that several men were killed and wounded, I yet feel thankful to her in that the "bull-ring" was no more. Not that one could quite escape it, for always it was used for gas drill, and at Étaples that was "some stunt". Without warning, gas bombs were dropped among the men who would be listening to a lecture on gas, and the shout "gas!" would go,

---

2   Martin Gilbert: "...there had been an incident behind the lines (early September, 1917), at Étaples...Scuffles broke out in the town between soldiers and the military police, the disturbances spread, and the camp commandant and a dozen officers were thrown into the river...When further disturbances broke out on 12th September, 1917, aimed at the much disliked Mititary Police, reinforcements were called in and a cavalry brigade alerted. But when concessions were made to the men, and the rigours of training relaxed, calm was restored. The British "mutiny" had been a muted one. When, however, Chinese labourers at Étaples demanded better conditions, their protest was suppressed by troops without compunction, or compassion."

and there was a scurry to get the mask on before there was any damage done. It was a good training, but not a pleasant one.

After the soldiers had gone through the "bull-ring" they drew the last of their trench kit, and looking more like pack mules than human beings, commenced the journey to the Divisional Wing for the Unit to which they had been posted. After more taming at the Wing they went on to the Unit, where they were met by the Regimental Sergeant-Major, who proceeded to "liven them up" before detailing to their various companies. There each man went before the Company Sergeant-Major who sent him to his platoon, the sergeant of which allocated him to his section, and then at last he could rest—after many months a "fighting unit in a fighting mob."

VI
NEARER A PICTURE OF HELL THAN ANY MORAL HAS YET CONCEIVED
13TH MARCH, 1920

THE BATTALION to which I was posted was, at the time of my joining them, in the Ypres sector. Everybody has heard of Ypres, and a very great number of local soldiers have been in that sector at one time or another. To those who have only heard of Ypres, it represents a much shelled town and a severely "strafed" Cotton Hall, for the destruction of which the Germans were to be severely dealt with, first by the arms of the Allies and then by a thundering indemnity. To those who have been there under war conditions, it is the most accursed place in all the battle area, and that means in all the world. Writers of real ability and with fluent and facile pens have endeavoured to picture this devastated waste of mud and have failed miserably. I am not going to attempt to describe it. Of the town I saw practically nothing, and of the salient far more than enough, though I was there only a brief period. The place is thrice accursed to me, for here it was first that I had my good, clean uniform vilified with the mud from which it was seldom afterwards clear; here it was that I made my first intimate acquaintance with the vermin which were thereafter my constant companions in prosperity and adversity, in victory and defeat; here it was too that I first learned the real meaning of "barrage" and learned of the spitefulness of inanimate things; and here it was that I first went "over the top."

I think that, in my Army experience, I have heard every "swear word" there is, from those which are as antiquated as sin itself to those which were newly coined to meet the exigencies of war, including the choice blend used on all possible and impossible occasions by our forceful Colonials; and embracing the Yankee brand which does not lack body, and if all were collected together in one volume and strung one after the other, and ending with the word Ypres, that would, to a small extent give those who were not there, an idea of what Ypres was like. It was an intensive casualty culture area, and in times of stress, when either one or the other side was attacking, it was much nearer a picture of Hell than any mortal has yet conceived. The ground in this area was waterlogged, so the trenches could not be dug; and our protection consisted of the scrapings of a few feet of earth down, thrown up on top to make a wall of sufficient height to shelter under. This meant of course, that there could be no "dug-outs" or shelters (I mean actual coverings for soldiers in wet or cold weather) so that the troops holding the line had to lie, to all intents and purposes, in the open. In fine weather—I was not there in the fine weather season—it must have been bad; in wet weather it was unspeakably miserable; with frost—well, I'm thankful to say I was away in another sector before I had to endure it.

These trenches—lines of shell holes and scraped up earth—were, when I was there, in a nice, slimy condition. If one touched anything, and one could not but be without doing so, some of the mud stuck, and soon one had a large collection of Ypres mud all over one's person. To add to the pleasantness of the prospect, all around were dead men in all stages of decomposition, and even bits of men were strewn here and there. Some of these had never been buried, some had been, but their last rest had been disturbed and a shell had unearthed the body or part of it. After wholesome training camps of Britain and a wholesome Base Depot, this sort of thing came as an unpleasant shock, and my constant wish from then on was that peace might come swiftly, or that I might get a "Blighty one," and get out of it all. To add to the general unpleasantness there was a continual growl of artillery and the rapping of machine guns, with their consequent concert of whining shells, and hissing bullets, a fearsome din concluding with nerve-rending reports as the shells burst.

I may digress here a minute to say that, when I was at the Divisional Wing awaiting transference to the Battalion to which I was posted, I used to go out of the hut in the darkness of the evening to watch the horizon lighted up with the flashes of the firing guns. I was too far away to hear the reports, but all the horizon was kept an almost continuous angry red with the gun flashes, and I used to yearn to get there "where things were being done." My yearning for the Divisional Wing was far greater when I had been "in the line" in the salient for about half-an-hour!

I met, before I went to France, a Shetlander who had been wounded several times, and who had been home on draft leave prior to "going over" to "collect another bit of Jerry's shrapnel," as he put it. We met on a train, and he told me he was last hit in Ypres. He also told me about Ypres, and the more he spoke of the horrors of it, the more enthusiastic I felt, and the keener to get there and see what it was like. We are built that way. When we hear of some great discomfort, or great danger, and actually meet some who have undergone it, we immediately feel keen to go through it. But when we get to it and find out that discomfort is really uncomfortable and that danger is really unhealthy, we grumble and want to get away from it with the speed of aeroplanes. So it was with me. To hear of the mud and of this soldier jumping into a shell hole at night for shelter from the lethal missiles of the Hun only to find out, when it became light enough, that he had as companions two dead men; and to hear of him "collecting bits of shrapnel" filled me with enthusiasm; but to feel the mud sticking to my legs and clothes, to smell the dead in their shell holes, and to feel that the next shell was sure to drop on me and make me like the chap we met as we were coming in—a big man with his leg shattered near the hip, moaning almost inaudibly, and with his face that peculiar greenish yellow which pallor under tan gives—well, all these things made me regret my keenness and displaced it with a sudden desire to see home again and a "civvy" suit.

The collection of vermin was very simple. One went to a section of which most of the members had been in the country for a considerable time, one drew blankets and "turned in," slept the night, and woke up verminous. Thereafter it was impossible to be clean. One did one's best. Whenever possible, he had baths and clean changes; he also used creosote freely on the clothes he couldn't change; he had those clothes fumigated and he used all sorts of preparations guaranteed to kill vermin, besides having thorough searches at all possible times. The best result he could hope for was say an hour's peace. The kilt had some advantages. It was cool in the summer and kept the back warm in the winter, but it was incredibly verminous all the year round. All this is no doubt very unpoetical and unexciting, but is horribly true, and it is one of the only sure things in war. Whenever anyone waxes enthusiastic about war, be it verbally or in print, always recollect that the honour and glory are thickly salted with lice, and if he is talking, tell him about it, while if it is in print make a note of it. It is probably quite true that beneath every uniform on active service there beats a brave heart and one willing to shed its life-blood for the cause his country says is just—whatever the country is or whatever the cause— but there also beat a few thousand hearts beneath that tunic which are causing that soldier torment you wot not of. Honour and glory! Vermin and mud! The first is what they told us of—the second is what we experienced.

VII
"OVER THE TOP, LADS, AND THE BEST OF LUCK!"
20TH MARCH, 1920

ALTHOUGH WE—the Division to which I was attached—were practising "stunts" all the time, we were out of the line at Ypres, we were told, for what reason I do not know, that we should rest assured that we were not going over the top. Even when we came into the line preparatory to going over, we were told that we would not have to leave our trench. On the night before the attack we were told that we might have to go over, but in all probability we would not; we would only have to advance if the troops going over failed to take their objective. When we "stood to" on the morning of the attack we were informed that we were actually going forward with the rest of the attackers! We learned afterwards that it was known, when the plan of attack was formulated, that our Division[3] was going to take part, but why the men who were actually going should have been kept in ignorance of this is a mystery I have never been able to understand. There was certainly no chance of desertion, and I do not think that the knowledge that we were going to stay in a trench until the attack was over could have had any good effect on the soldiers, as they knew that, if they did not take part in the storming of the enemy trenches, they would have to sustain the shock of any counter-attacks the enemy might attempt, or else, worse still, take occupancy of the enemy trenches captured, with the knowledge that the work of consolidation would fall heavily on them, and the certainty of coming in for more than a full share of the spiteful "strafing," meted out to those unfortunates who held a captured trench, on which, naturally, the enemy artillery could work with great accuracy. However, we had to go over, which was the main thing.

When we came up the line, the artillery fire was very intense. Both sides were hammering away at each other with great enthusiasm. I may mention that on this front the artillerymen of both sides had ample gunfire practice, all hours of the day and night being made hideous with the continual thunder of all calibres of artillery, the shriek of the passing shells, and the thuds of their detonation. This was merely intensified at the time of which I speak, but to me, who was ignorant of what warfare really meant, and to whom this was an initiatory experience, it was beyond description. As we "stood to," immediately prior to going over, our barrage opened up. The din to which I had been listening, seemed a comparative silence to the noise now. There was a huge thunderous report as every gun went off and the air seemed to be full of the shriek and whine of shells, carrying death and destruction to our friend the Hun, while the air throbbed with the rat-tat-tat of machine guns and hissed with the passing bullets. Almost immediately our barrage started the German guns replied, all sorts and sizes of shells bursting all round, close at hand and in the distance. It was a nerve-wracking ordeal and I do not believe there was anyone on the wide front of the attack but felt the strain. It was, it must be remembered, still dark, though the continuous flash of the guns lit up the night sky as far as the eye could see, and the nearer darkness was punctuated with the burst of shells. I could quite understand the statement that the contour of the ground changed quickly where there was much shell fire.

Very soon after the barrage opened, and before we left our trench, I heard that most pitiful cry—"Stretcher-bearers!" and saw the two nearest hurrying along with a stretcher to pick up the first of our casualties. But we were not given much time to think. An officer and a sergeant came hurrying along telling us to get ready, keep our heads and keep our rifles up and not let them be choked with mud, see that the magazines were full and the safety catch back, and our bayonets all right, see that our bombs were handy, and so on.

---

3 For the duration of the war, the 2nd Seaforths were attached to the 4th division.

Then the officer took his place and the sergeant stood with him, while the former counted off the time before we were to go forward. Then "Over the top, lads, and the best of luck!" and we were away. We scrambled out over the heaped up dirt that was our parapet, and were glad to get moving. The suspense of the last few seconds was terrible, waiting, waiting, and all the time feeling the very ground tremble with the shock of the explosives as the shells fell all round, hearing in a dim sort of way, the cries of the wounded, and knowing that once beyond that parapet there was nothing to save one but his luck. The movement forward was a relief beyond words.

It should not be thought that soldiers go over the top, shrieking battle-cries and with their rifles at the charge. Far from it. Perhaps that was the method earlier in the war—probably it was; but with the coming of trench warfare that changed. The soldiers "slung" their rifles, and strolled forward—with an eye to alignment—calling to each other, and practically every man with a newly lit cigarette in his mouth. No sooner were we over than men began to drop, and those who were able immediately threw everything and bolted for the aid post. Those who were not able lay still, some calling for stretcher-bearers, and some shrieking with pain and excitement. But the rest hurried on, not callously, but because, in an attack, there is no time to attend to anyone but the enemy, and the infantry-man's first duty is to do that. There are stretcher-bearers to look after the wounded, and the wounded have to take their chances until the stretcher-bearers can get to them.

So we went on, thinned a little, and came to the first line of the enemy. Then we started to run, charged, and shouted, threw a bomb or two, and jumped into the enemy trench. The barbed wire in front had been severely dealt with by the artillery, so that our passing was comparatively easy, and those Germans who did not surrender, considerably bolted, so that we had the trench without a great struggle. Then on again. We came to the second trench and entered it in much the same way, but we were less fortunate here, for we had hardly got into it when the Germans launched a counter-attack in force and promptly drove us out. We had a good number of casualties here, and we were driven back a considerable distance before we steadied and went back. (I may mention that a German attack had been arranged to take place either on this day or the day following; hence the large number of men collected here ready to launch the counter-attack.)

It was daylight by this time and we went forward again. The German counter-attackers suffered heavily in the open from our Lewis guns and from our artillery, and there was little fight in them when we went for them. We took most of them prisoners and on we went, till finally, we took our objectives, when we, a greatly reduced Company—and, as learned afterwards, a greatly reduced Battalion—set to consolidate and hold our line against attacks. All the time, it should be remembered, the shell-fire did not diminish, and the machine gun bullets whizzed through the air literally in thousands. We had two small, half hearted counter-attacks before noon, but the Germans never reached our line, and suffered pretty severely in coming the distance they did.

Naturally, this day is somewhat chaotic to me. Certain things I remember with great distinctness. For instance I remember seeing a big German with a black moustache, like the Kaiser's, sitting in the mud and looking stupidly at his foot, which was not there, having been blown off, leaving the leg of the knee-boot which he was pulling up, though it could go no further. I remember seeing a large "strong point"—a concrete house with a steel door—crowded with wounded men, Germans and British, taking shelter from the heavy shell-fire. I saw four Englishmen carrying a stretcher containing a wounded man, and a shell came and killed or wounded (I don't know which) all the bearers, who dropped, and the stretcher, of course, also dropped, and the wounded man dived—that is the only word that can describe it—from it into the mud. It would have been amusing had it not have been so tragic. I saw two Germans, both young, tall, slim-built, lying together, dead, one holding a machine gun in his arms and the other lying across his legs. I saw one of our sergeants get hit in the arm, turn an astonished face to those near him, and get a rifle or machine gun bullet in his head, I saw, as we passed along, little groups of dead or wounded, big groups of badly wounded men. And I do not yet understand how anybody got through alive, nor can I understand how any got through unhit.

I think it was two days afterwards when we were relieved. I know I was tired, dirty, sleepy, miserable, hungry and sore, and not at all elated that I had been a factor in a glorious victory. I became more cheerful as we left the noise and shell-fire behind, and much more cheerful after some hot food and a good sleep. But I did not even then, and I do not yet feel any pride in the share I had in that or any other attack. Victory—even defeat—can be made to look romantic on paper, but the experience of one who took part in both is that there is no romance in it, only sorrow and hard work, hunger and dirt, and a great desire to get back to the time when one was a very ordinary "civvy" in a very ordinary job.

I may mention here, that in the official account of this attack, it was announced that the British casualties were slight. There were some 60 English and Scottish Battalions, together with Welsh, Irish, Australian and New Zealand, which took part, and our stretcher-bearers were absent from five to eight days collecting wounded! This can give one an idea of what constituted "slight" casualties. We should be very thankful we never had any official "heavy" casualty lists.

VIII
THE SPIRIT OF COMRADESHIP
27TH MARCH, 1920

SHORTLY AFTER our victory at Ypres we were removed to Arras where we received reinforcements and took over a sector of the line. Here we spent the whole winter, and we were tolerably fortunate in having such a good system of

1. The Bull-ring at Étaples: "a city founded on sand".

2. A church parade behind the lines on the Western Front.

3. Seaforth Highlanders Lewis Gun post, October, 1917.

4. Stretcher Bearers at Ypres, 1917: "the trackless waste, full of pitfulls and dangers..."

trenches to hold. The ground around this district is chalk, and the trenches were splendidly made, deep, and bottomed with trench boards. Here in the third and second lines were dug-outs of good depth, affording a sense of security in times of stress; but in the front line we only had shelters dug in the face of the trench, and often these were only raw earth without "plenishing" of any kind and always they were too small to contain the number of men allocated to them. The consequence was that we were packed together in these little holes, and, naturally, only managed to secure snatches of sleep when off duty. I might mention here that some officers did not approve of men sleeping in the front line and made a point of seeing that they did not; but in the Company of which I was a unit the officers were very reasonable and allowed us more sleep than they often themselves had.

I am going to endeavour to give you an impression I personally received of the spirit of comradeship engendered by the war. I am not going to give the name of the man who figures in the story but I may say he belonged to a country district in Aberdeenshire and that he was a farm servant who smoked thick black tobacco usually and had a marvellous vocabulary of oaths. I met him first in a training camp in Britain and I did not like him. He was immensely ignorant about everything but agriculture—a subject about which I knew nothing—so that we had little in common about which to converse, also he was a raw recruit while I had some months' training in and naturally felt my vast superiority; I objected to his pipe, and, not so much, to the language, with which he embellished practically every sentence he uttered, and I objected to his laugh, which was mostly an annoying splutter, and which was continually in evidence. Yet, for some reason or other, he picked me out as his friend. He came to me first with all the camp rumours, and even became so trustful of my abilities to indite a letter for him to the minister of the church of his parish to thank him for sending him some "comforts" and a letter, the reply to which, he explained, was "particular," and he was rather afraid his epistolary abilities could not cope with it. I obliged.

We went on leave at the same, and he travelled with me to Aberdeen. There he insisted on "standing" me a "feed," and he took me to a shop which made a speciality of hot "mealy puddings." I think he was sorry to leave me at a "loose end" in Aberdeen when he proceeded home. He was back on time and I was not. He met me, however, on the night of my arrival at the camp and was very solicitous about me, making anxious enquiries as to whether I had a good excuse to offer for my absence and whether I minded "doing time." If I had to "do time," however, he promised to see that I had cigarettes supplied me among my "grub." (It should be understood that prisoners and sick men in the camp hospital had their food brought to them from the hut to which they had been allocated). His offer to defy the military law, however, was never carried into effect as the excuse I had was considered sufficient, and I remained as free an agent as a soldier can be.

We crossed to France together, and went to Ypres together, and foregathered for the winter, as stated, at Arras. Through an oversight on one occasion, I went up the line without a sufficient supply of cigarettes, and, much to my horror, I discovered when it was our turn for the front line, that I had not a single "tab" left to soothe my jaded nerves. This Aberdonian, on this occasion, was not with the Company, but was with the cookers and had the job of carrying hot food to the troops, at least once a day. The weather was very cold, and these "orderly men" were looked for eagerly by everyone in the line—almost as eagerly as was the rum jar. It was not etiquette in the line for one soldier to "bone fags" from any but his nearest and dearest pal, and even that was not really "good form," because cigarettes were sometimes very scarce and a pal could hardly refuse a cigarette even though he knew that he was going to be short himself before Sunday, on which day the issue "came up." I endured two days without a cigarette and on the night of the second I determined to take my courage in both hands and ask for one. I happened to be off duty when the evening hot meal came up. The soup—for soup it usually was—was usually carried in some sort of thermos flask arrangement strapped to the back of the orderly man. The man who had adopted me as a pal duly came up, and swung off his receptacle, and immediately there was a rush by the men in the section off duty to have their canteens filled. When I had seen to filling my canteen I went across to my friend—though I had never really felt friendly toward him—and sheepishly asked if he had a spare "fag." He unearthed a packet containing one—his last—which he offered me. Hungry as I was for a smoke I could not accept so generous an offer as that, though he reminded me that he "aye had his pipe." I asked him to show me his tobacco, but, after telling a white lie about having it at the cookers, he admitted that he had none, but prophesied that he would easily be able to get some from the chaps at the cookhouse. I knew better, however, and refused to rob him. Even then he offered me half the cigarette, but I sorrowfully refused and returned to my "cubby-hole" to discuss my soup and despair about ever winning the war when a man could be left without a cigarette for two whole days!

With a cheery "good night, lads, and good luck," the soup man departed, and turning a corner, was out of sight in a few seconds. Hardly had he disappeared, however, than three trench mortars came over in quick succession and the voice of my pal almost simultaneously for assistance. We dropped our soup and ran round the corner to find him lying down. It was pitch dark, of course, so that we could not see what exactly was the matter, though it did not take a Sherlock Holmes to know that he was a casualty. We soon found out what had taken place, however, as we sent the word down for stretcher bearers. My friend had been hit in the back, and his left arm was almost torn off. The receptacle for the soup was torn open, and the hot liquid had run down his back, scalding the lower part of his body and his legs. As we stood there awaiting the stretcher-bearers, I bent over him and spoke to him. His pain-twisted face cleared a little and he indicated his pocket. "Tak' the fag," he said, "I'll no' need it." He died in a few minutes—before the stretcher-bearers arrived, in fact, and they did not dally on the way.

I have often wondered since then what I would have done under the circumstances. Here was an ignorant, so far as education went, farm servant, wounded unto death, and apparently aware of the fact, thinking not of himself or his wounds or even his imminent death, but of the man he had made his pal, and of that pal's desire for a cigarette! One never can tell what one will do under certain circumstances, but I should not care to bet that one in a thousand would have so acted as did the man who, if I never made a friend of him in life, became one of my dearest friends in his dying.

IX
EXPOSURE
3RD APRIL, 1920

I PROMISED when I began that I had no intention of writing a chronological history of the war, and from this point on the sequence of the incidents of which I write will be most noticeable by its absence. The reason for this must be obvious. War is naturally chaotic and the experiences endured by the soldier do not come to his mind like a roll of cinematograph film, but in chaotic cameos on a general background of noise, dirt, discomfort and ennui. I am going to endeavour, therefore, to give the cameos, not as they actually occurred as to time, but as they occur to my mind, though I have no power to inspire my pen-pictures with the realities seared on the minds of all who, joining up to strike a blow for freedom, discovered the limitations of the heart-warming flame of patriotism and came to know that the honour and glory they heard about before they donned khaki existed only on the safe side of the field of battle, and not in actuality.

There is a great deal of talk at present, not only locally, but all over Scotland, about "Pussyfoot" and the chances for ridding that country of its thirst for the national beverage by legislation[4], and I do not wish readers to use the following article either for or against the campaign. It only goes to prove one thing and that is that, whether or not alcoholic liquors should be removed from every person in a position to supply them, they should find a place in the doctor's dispensary and in the chemist's shop.

It was very cold weather in the early part of the year and wet snow had been making life very disagreeable for the soldiers holding the line. It was on the second day on this occasion, and at night three of our company were picked to occupy an observation post out in front of our front line. Those soldiers who know the Arras front will perhaps remember the section which enters below Monchy-le-Preux. The front line ended there in a dead end; really a part of the line had been disused and had silted up; and the last post on this sector was some ten yards from the dead end. They may also perhaps remember that the last ten yards of trench were not very well looked after, so that the parapet was

---

4   The American National Prohibition Act became law at midnight on 16th January, 1920.

low, and the bottom was somewhat uneven. At the end of the trench a piece of tape guided the unfortunate observation post men to the shell hole which was to be their home for the 24 hours and which certainly offered no shelter from the elements. Added to this lack of shelter was the fact that no hot food could be prepared there and at night no cigarettes could be smoked. The job of holding this post was not competed for with any great enthusiasm, and there was a decided reluctance to take up this duty in winter.

The three men chosen for duty on the night of which I speak received their instructions, which included a rather, as it proved, ironic order not to sleep, and they moved off when darkness set in to relieve the tenants of the shell hole. The night, of course, was inky dark, and all around the ground was "soppy" with the wet snow, and the men, of course, were not dry. As they proceeded up the trench they were challenged at each post by the muffled figure of a sentry looming large in the darkness, whose miserable voice only accentuated their own misery as they thought of these "lucky devils" with their "two hours on and four off" and their little "cubby holes" for shelter. As they passed the last post they got warning that this had a big hole between that post and the end of the trench, but no warning of where it actually was nor how to negotiate.

With a muttered grumble at almost every step they went forward, when "splash" and number one was floundering out at the other side of a hole full of water and wet snow which had taken him up to the waist (the hole, of course, looked solid enough in darkness). Numbers two and three halted and looked round to see how they could get across dry, while number one swore audibly. Number two tried one side of the hole, but was also unfortunate enough to drop in, while number three had no better luck, though he gingerly felt all round the hole to see if he could find a foothold, the other two raising a hymn of hate against the Germans, the British, this particular sector, the troops who had last held the trench and left the hole unfilled, and number three for keeping them standing about. In due course, however, he literally followed them and added his voice to the general lamentation. And as they arrived at the trench, and picked up the tape, they finally arrived at the shell-hole.

The night improved splendidly and a keen frost set in. You all know the pleasures of a dark, frosty night—the quick walk home from work, the warm up, and the mellow light, with the anticipation of a warm bed. Now I should like you to try and picture yourself, reader, in the place of any of these three men, soaked to the waist, wearing wet kilts, and greatcoats, boots and "hosetops", sitting in a shell-hole within hearing distance of the German front line and cut off from their own line, the shell-hole more than ankle deep in mud and wet snow, with not even the opportunity of a smoke, much less a warm drink. They spent surely the most miserable night of their lives. The frost gripped their wet clothes and, without any opportunity of moving about, gently punched each other to keep their blood circulating. Their "hosetops" froze to their legs—and that can be excessively painful—and their kilts froze. They "broke" the edges of their kilts and rubbed their legs, but mostly they moaned in their agony. For agony it was to become from painfully cold to numb. The long night dragged through its weary hours and daylight came, but it brought no relief. The very marrow of the bones seemed frozen. They were too miserable even to eat, though they smoked a few cigarettes throughout the day. They warmed their chill hands by opening their tunics and pressing them on their bare chests, but this only robbed the body of the little heat it had and did not really warm the hand. Finally, they crowded together and waited longingly for night again and its relief. They even joked a little among themselves about their instructions not to sleep, but their smiles were wry smiles, though each consoled the other with the happy idea that this was sure to cause frost bite and permanent relief from the trenches!

At last the relief came. It was again dark and still freezing. The three found, when they tried, that they really could not get up, and, when assisted, could not stand. Their legs and feet were quite numb and useless. The new men sent back for assistance, and six men arrived to help the frozen trio back to the line. Fortunately they met the Company Sergeant-Major (I may say that a W.O. seldom came up the line, but this one, a fine fellow and a gallant soldier, always shared the difficulties of his men, but, unfortunately, was wounded when he had been with us a short time). With characteristic and forceful brevity he asked what was the matter, and when informed gave instruction that the men should be taken to a dug-out in the second line. Meantime he went and saw the C.O. of the company, and they duly arrived and examined the men, who had to be put into a dug-out held by a trench-mortar gun crew, who had a brazier burning and a brew of tea in preparation. When the tea was ready, the Sergeant-Major produced a jar of rum, and with a liberal hand gave each of his soldiers a "double tot." A drink of hot tea followed, and all three men were fast asleep inside ten minutes. They were also excused fatigues for that night! All pain has its compensations. They woke up their own men next day, cold, naturally, for they were still wet, but knowing they were still cold which was better than being frozen numb. A pair of dry socks made new men of them, though I regret to say that neither of them got frost bite and all had to "carry on" till one was killed, one was wounded, and the other was demobilised.

What I wanted specially to say in this was that, had it not been for the rum these men received I have no doubt but that they all would have died. In fact, I know that would have been, and I know because I was one of those three.

X
FATIGUE
17TH APRIL, 1920

MUCH HAS been made in the press of the attacks and gallant stands against attack made by the British soldiers, and the stirring stories always unfolded had, I have no doubt, a very material amount to do with the willingness with which young fellows, who should have been in no more dangerous position than is occasioned on a fast football match, came forward to fill the blanks left by the result of these attacks and stands, and that despite the fact that, in the later years of the war, men discharged for wounds and men undergoing treatment in hospital were quite numerous to deter anyone, with an eye to future responsibilities, from entering the Army. Leaving aside all the little things that the press did not think worth mentioning in relation to the life of the man in khaki, there was one phase of the campaign that merits an article to itself, a phase that, had it received the ventilation it deserved during the war, would have acted as so effective a deterrent that the Conscription Act would have come much sooner than it did, and the great majority would have waited for their "papers," and then, if possible, "dodged the column". That phase can be summed up in the one word "fatigues," and I shall endeavour to give you a pen-picture of a typical fatigue in the winter time. But first, I would make it clear that attacks, either by ourselves or the enemy, were not of an everyday occurrence, nor was excitement in the line prevalent as a general thing. Quite the reverse. A monotony that corroded the soul hung over the soldier, from the day he joined his unit until the day he left, and that monotony was only occasionally enlivened by the excitement of attacks either by his unit or by the enemy, and the excitement, far from being exhilarating, was a long drawn out nightmare of terror, the only compensation to which was the sense of relief, when things quietened, to find that one was still alive, not a prisoner, and complete as to limbs, etc. And that sense of relief was a thing that had to be experienced to be understood. It is, so far as my experience goes, the most exquisite of all sensations "here below."

The Battalion had come out of the line, had landed at the camp early in the morning, and had had a good sleep, and a good breakfast. The men had begun to clean away the traces of the past week of dreary vigil, their rifles had been inspected, and they were taking sufficient interest in life to wonder if they were going to be "paid out." Everybody had that restful feeling of content that even a brief spell out of the trenches can bring. Then comes that bug-bear of all soldiers, that most hated of men, who even "while on the job," hates himself, the Orderly Sergeant—usually a full corporal. Cheerfully he enters the hut— the Battalion, being in the Mouchy-le-Preux sector of the Arras front, would naturally be in Wilderness Camp, which consisted of Army huts—and murders the new-born joy in the hearts of his hearers by announcing that "the following men will parade at 3.30 this afternoon for fatigue up the line." Follows a list of the names. It was at moments such as these that one noticed how well-named Wilderness Camp was. It stood in what had once been "no man's land,"—a desolate place, in a little hollow, lonely and lifeless, making the wilderness seem more deserted by its presence. It was like the light from a match on a very dark night—the darkness is only accentuated.

All the men picked for fatigue have valid reasons why they should not go on, but their excuses are magnificently swept aside, and with a regal, "It's got to be done boys," the Orderly Sergeant leaves the hut, followed by the impressive vituperations of sundry of the more loquacious of the fatigue men, to carry his message of blasted repose to the next hut. With the stains of the mud still wet upon them from their last "spell" of the trenches, these men, not yet fully recovered from the weariness of their ceaseless watching, their brief snatches of sleep, and the actual physical effects of the fatigues they had wrought when "up the line," fall in for an early tea, get on their equipment –"battle order"—and fall in at the "stand at ease." A Second Lieutenant and a Sergeant take charge, the officer brings the men to the slope, and the party marches off. "March at ease is given" as they leave the camp, and they are on the road.

The afternoon is dry, and the boys swing along, smoking and singing, cheerful and unthinking but of the moment as it is. So they progress, mile after mile, till the song gradually dies away and the cheerfulness vanishes, the darkness begins to fall, and, having left the main road, they stumble in the darkness, emitting their little growls and imprecations. They wonder about the fatigue and ask what it is. No one knows. Some Engineer fatigue. The Engineers come in for a full measure of violent criticism, and, apostrophising the Universe, several desired to know why the much adjectived Engineers can't do their own much adjectived work; they get all the money (also much adjectived), all get all the "cushy" jobs! According to the information I gathered from these scraps of conversation on the way to an Engineers' fatigue, I have no doubt that, next war, the Engineers are going to be the first Corps for recruiting.

The fatigue party enter the trenches. It comes on rain—it always did when one was on fatigue—and the men, doggedly now, march on, catching their feet on broken trench boards, coming up hard against the walls of trenches at the turns, scraping past men on duty and incidentally collecting more mud, getting wet and cold and miserable, tired already and with the knowledge that somewhere, probably in the front line, an Engineer—perhaps an officer, but more probably a lance-corporal—waits with a few hours' work for each man. Why can't Fritz put one over and give a chap a Blighty one? Thoroughly "fed up" the party arrives at the appointed place. What sort of a fatigue is it? Get spades! Digging fatigues! The spades are forthcoming, and the men each get a section; probably the job is to dig a space—"barm" is, I think, the technical name—between the trench top, the surface of the earth, and the parapet, the earth thrown up from the earth left in digging. The reason for this space is obvious—it hinders the loose earth from falling into the loose trench. The way one knew one had reached the trench-top was by the fact that he came on hard ground, or, as the Engineers put it, he "touched bottom." The fatigue is begun.

Mounted on the top of the trench each man, already weary and ready for real rest, starts to dig. Usually, when a man starts to dig, he throws off his jacket, and, if necessary, his waistcoat. The soldier on active service, on the other hand, is allowed to lay down his rifle—within instant reach of his hand—and that is all. Clad, as usual, with his greatcoat on and his equipment hampering his every movement, in a darkness that could be felt, in a drizzling rain and almost broken in spirit, he had his section to dig, and this he had to finish with the knowledge, too, that the whole party had to wait on the slowest man. The earth—it is winter—is soft and refuses to let go the shovel when it is dug in, and, when it is lifted, refuses to leave the shovel. Every spade thrust is a muscular effort, every "throw" an appreciable piece of work. Added to the natural clogginess of the soil is the fact that, here and there, one comes upon pieces of sand-bag work, where a shovel is no use, where one has to use his hands to pull the sand-bag from its sticky bed and heave it over. Occasionally one strikes rocky soil, where the shovel has had to be reinforced by a pick to break it up, when the shovel has had to be utilised once more. And all the time the rain falls and the darkness presses upon one till it is smashed by a flare, to close down darker than ever. There is no chance of seeing how the work is progressing. One must feel with one's hand to find out that. Oh, to get away from this eternal mud! God! For a machine-gun bullet in the leg or the arm! Surely it would be better even to be killed than to suffer like this every day. When will the war end? Why doesn't Jerry come over and give a chap a chance to go back a prisoner! Curse all wars. What a life! Dig, dig! Mud to the elbows, mud everywhere. And aches in every bone and muscle. Why the—wasn't I born on a farm or somewhere where digging was an essential part of the daily routine? How can they expect a man who never pushed anything heavier than a light wheelbarrow to push six yards of France back six feet? Dig, dig! So the hours crawl past, and at length the fatigue is completed, even the slowest man has completed his task, and the Engineer has inspected the work and growled that "it will have to do."

Then back to the Camp, through the trenches, with the rain persistently falling, the mud adhering, slipping on the damp trench boards with muddy feet, staggering and swearing. Everybody tries to hurry. The officer wants to get back to his hut and the sergeant wants to get back to his "bed," and they hurry along impatient at the lagging steps of the men who have sweated "on top", and who are naturally quite as keen on getting to bed as are their superiors. And so they come out of the trenches and on to the rough road that leads to the main road that leads to the camp. The warmth has left their bodies and they are cold, besides being tired and miserable. There is no singing now. Wet through, they stagger on, the main road is reached, and the camp within reasonable distance, it comes in sight! "All right, boys, just get inside," says the officer, as he runs off to make his report. The boys get to their huts, throw off their equipment and great-coats, and are greeted with the gladsome news that "there is a feed for the fatigue party." Hot tea, perhaps sausages! The orderly men fetch it in, there is a lifting of spirits as the food and warm tea disappears, and a general scramble "to get down to it" on the floor. Perhaps there are blankets. Then, indeed, are we luxurious. Off go the muddy boots and putties, and soon the hut is full of tired, contented, sleeping men, who reek not that to-morrow—no, to-day; for it is now morning—after the mud has been cleaned off, the rifles inspected, and the question of pay debated, the Orderly Sergeant will "come again," and they will pray devoutly for one machine-gun bullet or a little bit of shrapnel.

XI
UNDER THE VENEER OF CIVILISATION
24TH APRIL, 1920

I HAVE given in previous articles some idea of the life of the ordinary Tommy in most of its aspects. There is really very little to tell. It was, as I have said several times before, a life of dreary monotony, a squalid, dirty, brutalising life, with only the hope of a "cushy" wound, the half-fear, half-desire to be taken prisoner, and the terror (or hope, depending on one's personal outlook) of a serious wound, or fatal wound, to keep the mind from ceasing to function entirely, and becoming a mechanical arrangement for regulating mechanical movement. There was never much hope of the war ceasing. And perhaps the one thing that could do more in a brief hour to brutalise a man and make him disgusted with war and himself was the earnest use of the bayonet.

It should not be thought that the use of the bayonet was an everyday affair. Some soldiers, in fact, were fortunate enough to go through the latter portion of the war and never see it in use. But those who went earlier must have used it frequently, and a very great many must have had to put into actual practice the bayonet exercises they learned at home at least once. The bayonet, on active service, was almost a permanent fixture to the rifle, but not withstanding that it was the exception rather than the rule, even in attack or defence, that it came into "play." Naturally it could only be used when men were very close to each other, and I found, in the majority of cases, that, when we attacked, the enemy did not linger in a trench when we "arrived," but promptly surrendered or "cleared out," though always where there were dug-outs some went there and remained there until "coaxed" out by a hand grenade. When we were attacked in our turn, usually, the German wave was well broken before they reached our line, or we had instructions to "skin out" before the wave was upon us and retire to a second line where, more concentrated, we were able to smash any sort of wave he might send across. However, unfortunately, on occasion it was actually necessary to "mix up" in a bayonet fight, and on these occasions one soon found out what was under the veneer of civilisation.

A good deal has been said and written about gallant bayonet fights. There is nothing gallant about them. They are exceedingly unpleasant and very costly usually. I should think, though I cannot say with certainty, that the side with the most bayonets should win. I cannot say because one does not have time to see which side has most men, though on all occasions, owing to the fact that one is only sure of his immediate neighbours, the enemy seems to be very much stronger than the side he happens to be on. When a party of men were outnumbered, however, and had to have recourse to bayonets either to fight their way back to their unit or to save themselves from annihilation, the gallantry displayed was not the gallantry of a patriotic courage, but the gallantry of desperation. Of course, it might be said that they could have surrendered. That was not always possible. Modern warfare is swift and terrible, and an enemy does not cease fighting suddenly to send across a party to parley with a body of men they have at their mercy, nor have the surrounded or outnumbered men the opportunity of sending out a man under a white flag to offer to surrender. I question very much whether any body of men could have mustered a white flag among them had they wished to. Personally I saw two white flags while I was at the front. On one occasion three Germans, attacking us, took shelter in a house across a canal. A trench mortar was "put on" to the mark, and landed a shell through the roof. One man dived out of the house and into a shell-hole where he arrived at the same time as the second shell. The other two men got a sheet fixed to a piece of wood and shoved it out of the window. Before the trench mortar crew could be communicated with, however, the house was no more and the two prisoners were, I presume, "missing." The other occasion on which I saw the white flag was when a party of some 200 Germans were marching through a fire-swept zone in charge of a single Canadian private. They carried a tablecloth banner wise between two rifles, but I did not see the fire slacken any on account of this symbol of peace. So that, without wishing to detract any from the heroism of anyone who claims it, or for whom it is claimed, I would give it as my opinion that a bayonet fight was indulged in because there was nothing else for it, and not because the fighters felt a patriotic spasm and meant to add another lurid page to the history of his country.

One of the first things that strikes one in a bayonet fight is the absence of fire. When I say one of the first I should mention that he probably does not notice it at the time, but it dawns on him when he thinks about the matter afterwards. But there is an entire absence of fire, though as the fight eddies, someone with plenty of presence of mind may lob over a hand grenade or two among a group of his enemies when none of his own men is near enough to benefit by it. Also a rifle may occasionally be fired. But for the most part there is no firing though there is plenty of noise. Everyone is shouting, some because they are wounded, and some, wounded, because they are being trampled under foot, but most because they have been taught to shout to "keep their blood up." I have often heard it said that a man must be mad at the time he is bayonet fighting, or he could not fight. I don't think that is quite right, however. Some certainly are mad. I have seen a man cornered, and surrounded by a large number of Germans. He was a big man, and his eyes were blazing and he was "mouthing" and frothy. He was fighting like ten men, with lightning thrusts and parries, and he was certainly effective. He had his back to a trench corner, and he was literally heaping the dead round him. A German officer on the parapet went behind him and wounded him in the neck with a revolver bullet. He lived, however, and got the D.C.M. The officer was shot a few seconds later. He died, but he already had the Iron Cross. So that, though I would not say that all went berserk, still they got considerably "wound up" with excitement, and made a lot of noise. Still, they must keep a sufficiency of wits about them to use the bayonet properly, though, naturally, luck enters a great deal into the matter of getting through without injury. There are two places, leaving out arms and legs, where a bayonet is most effective, and that is the throat and the stomach. I had a trick from a French soldier which consisted of engaging the other man's bayonet and thrusting high. The result was "great" from my point of view. The German bayonet flew wide and mine went somewhere between his eye and the neck of his tunic. In falling he disengaged my bayonet and left me ready for the next man. It was a good trick and did not entail the hard work of thrusting a bayonet below a man's belt and withdrawing it quickly, with the risk of that man's bayonet puncturing one at the same time. There was always the risk too of sending the bayonet into his leather equipment and having it stick there, leaving a man practically unarmed and at the mercy of the man he was attacking, or of another man close at hand. Bayonet fighting was hard work and it was unlovely.

Needless to say, the bayonet in use soon became very messy, and this mess soon affected the rifle, so that it had that sticky, greasy feeling blood usually has. One's clothes too, already muddy, became spattered with blood, and the smell of blood pervaded everything. At the time of fighting that did not affect one to any great extent, but as soon as it was over, the effect was ghastly. One was literally overwhelmed with disgust. The blood caked to one's rifle and hands, and there was no chance of a wash. One had to eat with human blood on one's clothes, and, even after the hands had been rubbed and "scraped", there was blood under and around the finger nails. These were not pleasant meals. It is difficult, too, to get rid of the appearance of some of the men one was "up against", the look of terror and appeal, the twisted mouth. All these things, and the sight and sounds of the wounded, with their ghastly stabs and cuts, are not conducive to placid nerves and easy slumber. And this, I think, is why so many men sought forgetfulness in the wines of France when these were procurable. The brutalising effect of war generally, the murder of all the finer instincts by an animal-like existence, and the horrors endured by men that those at home might not conceive even in the shadow of that horror—these things, and not the meagre rum ration issued to the soldiers to keep their blood in circulation, were responsible for much of the drunkenness that prevailed among soldiers when opportunity offered. And those who are prone to blame them and to point the finger of scorn at them would do well to consider that, and try to understand that, if these soldiers have things to remember, there are also things they are glad to forget.

XII
"MAN, THAT'S WORSE
THAN BEING WOUNDED!"
1ST MARCH, 1920

PERHAPS IN dealing with the destruction caused by the war—the destruction caused to the men engaged in it, I mean—one does not understand very well the difficulties entailed in looking after the wounded, nor the number of hands a wounded man passed through before he was finally landed in a base, or better still a Blighty hospital. But part of this lack of understanding lies in the fact that the formation of a Division of troops is not fully understood. A Division is normally four Brigades, but, as a matter of fact, in the latter part of the war, a British Division consisted of three Brigades. Besides these Brigades there were the heavy and light artillery—R.H.A. and R.F.A., together with the Engineers and Army Service Corps. (There were also attached to each Division some aeroplanes, with their attendant officers and men, some stationary or observation balloons, with their complement of men, and some R.G.A. in charge of anti-aircraft guns. Of the arrangements for treating the sick and wounded of these I know nothing). There was also a Divisional Hospital, well back of the line, and to all intents and purposes, under ordinary circumstances, out of shell fire range. In each Brigade there were, besides a Field Ambulance, four Battalions (nominally for later it was reduced to three) and in each Battalion four Companies. Each Company had four (later three) platoons and each platoon four sections. In the Battalion there was also a Headquarters, consisting of men for special duties, drawn from all the Companies. All soldiers declare that all the Battalion Headquarters staff men had the "cushy" jobs, and the Company Headquarters men were only a little worse off. That did not hinder these soldiers, however, to be as loud and vehement in their condemnation of the war as the fighting soldier, and turn an envious eye to the men on Brigade and Divisional Headquarters. The Battalion Headquarters consisted of the signallers, police, sanitary corporal, aid post, transport, tailors, boot repairers, and in some cases, a "buckshee" or extra Lewis gun crew, and some special duty officers. (After the formation of a Machine Gun Corps, a Machine Gun Company was attached to each Brigade.) The Company Headquarters consisted of a few special duty men—the sanitary man, the Company stretcher-bearers, and a runner (messenger), etc. The stretcher-bearers of each Company numbered one man per platoon of four. It should be understood that the Headquarters men were not called upon to do fatigues, nor were they usually called upon to do sentry duty, though it was always necessary whenever two or three were gathered together, to have a gas sentry. I think I have now made it fairly clear how the troops were divided up, so that those that were not "over there" can have some idea that every infantry man was not necessarily a "front line soldier," and that the running of each Battalion was quite a little business in itself, complete in its minutest details, and with an Army Form or an Army Book to cover everything.

Now that I have made this roughly clear, I shall go on to the handling of the wounded, and shall endeavour to give my readers some impression of the life led by a Company stretcher-bearer. On an ordinary quiet day, a man who was unfortunate (or fortunate enough) to get wounded would naturally be in a trench. He himself or those near him would shout for stretcher-bearers, who would come up and see what the trouble was. If the wound was slight the man had to walk, and a slight wound might mean from a bullet through the fleshy part of the leg or arm to a compound fracture of the arm. If the wound was more serious the stretcher-bearers had to carry the man. First of all, of course, they had to put on a rough dressing. Then the man was lifted on the stretcher, and, with a man at each handle, the little party moved off in the direction of the Regimental Aid Post. It was no easy matter to carry a man through the tortuous trenches, where often the greatest difficulty was encountered in negotiating the corners, and I have seen a man being carried, roughly dressed, several hours on end, getting many a shake and jar, and gradually changing from a tanned groaning or swearing wounded soldier, to a practically lifeless, feeble, almost voiceless old man, with his face that greenish-yellow colour which paleness under tan gives. Arrived at the Aid Post, the stretcher-bearers hand over their charge and hurry back. The wounded man here receives the attention of the Medical Officer and his satellites—a corporal and probably two men who know something of first aid. When they have dressed the wound, and given the patient a hot drink and a cigarette, they hand him over to the stretcher-bearers supplied by the Brigade Ambulance—usually four in number to each Battalion—who take him to the Field Ambulance. If the times were quiet and the wound not too serious, the wounded man might remain there, but usually he was sent further afield, to a Stationary Hospital, and, in times of stress, when there were many wounded, from there to the Base, and thence, when fortune was in a good mood, to Blighty. At the Regimental Aid Post the man had a ticket attached to him detailing his wound. If it was a serious wound the ticket was red-edged, but if not serious, the ticket was white. This was to save time at the Field Ambulance. If he left the Field Ambulance he had another ticket attached, and so on till he got to Britain, each man being "classed" as to whether he was a deck patient or a stretcher case, etc. The same applied to Ambulance trains. I may mention that there were no sisters or nurses in a Field Ambulance, though there were some in a Stationary Hospital. At each place visited by the wounded man, his wound was examined and redressed, and he usually had something hot to drink and a smoke also. A soldier who was not too badly wounded was indeed a happy man!

In ordinary times the life of a stretcher-bearer was not a hard one. He had no rifle to carry (and consequently no rifle to keep clean), no bayonet and no ammunition. He had a stretcher and a bag of field dressings, but, most important of all, he had no fatigues—he dug not, neither did he carry barbed wire. When, however, there were even only a few wounded his life was not a happy one! If the men were wounded in the day time, he had the difficulty of carrying them through trenches, if at night he "risked life" and carried them over the trackless waste, full of pitfalls and dangers in the shape of shell-holes and stray shells and machine-gun bullets. Either way his task was a hard one. Added to this he had to "pick" his cases. He had to choose from among the wounded the most necessary cases first and so on. In the night time this was no easy matter, for the slighter the wound the more clamorous could be the patient. If the wounded were all together, he also had to dress them before taking any of them away. In the darkness this too was a difficult matter. I have seen a man, wounded below the knee, neatly bandaged above the knee, he being unable to "locate" the wound himself, and the stretcher-bearer doing so by the sense of touch—not an easy thing to do. If a wound was very serious, say, the most of the flesh being torn off the upper leg or a piece of shrapnel having torn a gaping wound in the chest, the stretcher-bearer could only lay on his dressing, and these, in the course of transporting the patient to the Aid Post, usually slipped off, leaving the wound bare. The stretcher-bearer too had to fight for his rights. Often a man not seriously hit would refuse to walk, and the stretcher-bearer had to bully him into going with a little assistance, for it should be understood that even to four men, a light man becomes heavy when most of his weight is borne on the wrists, as it was when a man was being carried through the trenches, or when the stretcher-bearers were wading in the mud of the ground "over the top", and continually slipping into shell-holes, the while endeavouring to save their charge from toppling off his stretcher. If the stretcher-bearer had a hard life dealing with the wounded in quiet warfare, in attack his existence was miserable. He ran exactly the same risk as his fighting comrades—at times even more for he had to loiter over the wounded, and could not dodge out and in to escape shell fire. The work had to be done all in the open, which was always strewn with shell fire, so that usually those wounded who could did not wait either for a stretcher-bearer or a dressing, but "slipped" everything and bolted for the Aid Post. This simplified matters for the stretcher-bearers, who could with safety pick up any men they found lying, dress him, and carry him off. Cases were always plentiful, and to show that the work was not light I may mention that one stretcher-bearer I knew had been absent 11 days after his Battalion had been withdrawn from the line, fetching in wounded belonging to that and other Battalions. During that time he had little sleep, and had been employed besides carrying wounded, in carrying food to them as they lay in the open. To show also that the work was not without danger I might explain that, on another occasion, one Company's stretcher-bearers had to be renewed three times—one man at a time, his predecessor having been killed or wounded.

I think I have written enough to show that the wounded were attended to as well as possible. The delay in attending to them always occurred when the stretcher-bearers, even when augmented for the purpose, could not cope with the numbers. I have never met a stretcher-bearer who refused duty or neglected a man who was wounded. They were always willing to do their best, though they had to work under the most adverse conditions and often at great personal hazard. They grumbled, of course, and the attention they bestowed on a wound was often negligible—I never saw a broken bone "splinted" in any way save once, and that time a crooked piece of branch had been fastened to a leg, badly damaged at the back of the knee, with a piece of telephone wire. The end of the branch slipped, before the man reached the Aid Post, so that it lay athwart the leg. It took a man the best part of half an hour to loosen the wire, and then, while one man held up the damaged leg, he had, by main force, to pull the branch from the raw wound. The patient, I am glad to say, was a hero. He never murmured till it was all over, when he said—"Man, that's worse than being wounded!" I have no doubt it was! It was a splendid demonstration of the adage about a little knowledge being a dangerous thing!

XIII
THE MEDICAL CROWD
8TH MAY, 1920

I HAVE DEALT more or less with the handling of the wounded, and with the life of the stretcher-bearer, and I shall now try to present the picture of a Regimental Aid Post. The "Post" consisted of anything available within a reasonable distance from the trenches, and was always behind the third line. Sometimes it was a dug-out, but more often a cellar, strengthened by the masonry that had fallen on it and by sandbags. The attendants in the Aid Post were the Battalion Medical Officer, a corporal and two or three privates. Earlier in the war these attendants were "lent" to the Battalion by the Brigade Field Ambulance, but later the R.A.M.C. men were replaced by men belonging to the Battalion. As in the case of every Battalion "job," the men picked were seldom chosen because of their knowledge of the work required of them, but for some occult reason only known to the officer who undertook to choose the men. I was fortunate enough to secure a job in our Battalion Aid Post soon after the R.A.M.C. men were withdrawn. I was chosen because I was at the time a stretcher-bearer and also because I knew some rudiments of first aid. With these qualifications I should have been selected for a cook or a policeman, but through some blunder I was picked for work about which I knew something. The corporal in charge was picked because he was a corporal and also because he was a 1914 soldier; another man was chosen because he was entitled to wear eight "wound bars," and the third because he had a weak heart.

Every Aid Post had an excellent supply of all that was necessary to enable one to deal with any case that might come from the Battalion, from a sick man to a mutilated hero, and the material was all stowed away and neatly labelled into two Field Medical Panniers, and in a small basket known among the Aid Post men as a "monkey box." We also had a water tester, with instructions for use. (We never used it). The two panniers had a Maltese cart in which to be borne to and from the line, but owing to the bulk of a horse and cart making too large a blot on the landscape and thus drawing enemy fire, the horse, cart and panniers were always left behind. Thus the Aid Post requisites were borne to and from the line on the backs of the "medical crowd." They also had to carry their own "battle order," but no rifle, bayonet or ammunition. That the Aid Post, our Aid Post, I mean—never ran short of dressings and other necessities for dealing with the wounded and sick says much for the backs of the Aid Post staff! While I was in the Aid Post, we conducted operations in a cellar, in a tin shed, in a dugout, and in the open trench, but not for long in the latter.

The Aid Post men were on Headquarters, and had no fatigues. In quiet times the life was grand. One had both the time and convenience to cook one's food and to have hot meals daily. One also had unlimited cigarettes—the "comforts" intended for the wounded, who came rarely—and one had the opportunity of an occasional wash and shave. One had also plenty of sleep. The police usually did gas sentry over the Aid Post so that the inmates thereof, when things were quiet, had nothing to do but play cards, eat and sleep, though there was always one man on duty all night. Seldom a day passed, however, but there was some wounded. They came mostly at night, and they came so that one could be attended to and sent off before another arrived. This meant a great deal, both to the men of the Aid Post and to the wounded themselves, because the latter could be sure of the best attention possible, and the former did not have to "rush" and consequently possibly "scamp" the work.

Most of the work, as I have said, came at night, so that we had to work by candle-light. I mention this, because we had, in one of the panniers, a lamp with shutters (so that the wounded could be dressed in the field, I presume), but I never saw the lamp in use. Candles gave a very good light in a small area, but they had their disadvantages. Before I mastered the art of holding a candle properly, I was constantly being "pulled up" for dropping candle grease into wounds or down the Medical Officer's tunic, or also for singeing the Medical Officer's hair or burning his face. In time I became proficient at collecting the grease in my hand and singeing nothing!

Like everybody's life over there, it could be very "full" for a stretcher-bearer. I shall give my readers some idea of my first attempt at "doctoring" a wounded man. There were two "raids" made from our side on the Germans, but on this occasion they did not, in the parlance of the soldier, "come off." The Germans were prepared, and only one man reached the German line. He was an officer and that was the last I heard of him. The raid was timed for early in the evening—it was dark, of course—and two hours after the men went over, an officer came into the Aid Post to tell us that it was a failure and to look for wounded. Shortly afterwards the first "case" came in. He had "stopped" a hand grenade. Half his foot was partially blown off, so that from the instep his foot "hinged" back, his toes lying on his sole. His ankle was badly damaged, and his legs literally peppered with small bits of steel. His hip on the same side was torn open, and his shoulder and arm on the same side were much torn and

5. "Nearer a picture of Hell than any mortal had yet conceived". The Ypres battlefield, 1917.

6. Exhausted Seaforth Highlanders stretcher-bearers, 29th August, 1918.

7. The 2nd Battalion Seaforth Highlanders form the Guard of Honour, 25th February, 1918.

8. Seaforth Highlanders Patrol moving forward, 29th August, 1918.

spattered with small scraps. This was the first occasion on which I had been in an Aid Post, and though I had been a stretcher-bearer and carried many wounded, I had never really examined a badly wounded man in the light. I became physically sick as I looked at him and could feel the sweat start from my forehead. The Medical Officer also saw how I was affected, and, having drastic methods of curing the softer feelings, forthwith picked me out to assist him to dress this patient. It had to be done and I did it, though that dressing took more out of me than anything else had done. I could not take a meal for several days after, and when I slept I kept dreaming of the wounds this man bore. However, it cured me of any squeamishness for the future, and I could always, after this, tackle any sort of wound and get a dressing fixed. On this occasion we had, if I remember, sixteen wounded to dress, and "clear"—send to the Field Ambulance—two of whom died, the first man in, and the last, who was shot through the upper leg, the bullet passing through the artery.

On another occasion, in a daylight raid, when I was more hardened to the work, we dealt with 56 wounded, including three Germans. These included some terrible wounds. An officer was carried in with a piece of shrapnel in his stomach—a most painful wound. His intestines were displaced, and hung inside the skin over his hips. He hardly murmured at his pain, and on his ticket being made out, impressed on the man making it that there was a hyphen between his last two names! A machine gun corps man came in with a large portion of his back blown away. He was put on a stretcher out of the way to die peacefully, and a man was sent to watch for his end. The Medical Officer came in and looked at him several times, and once, when the patient was lying with his eyes closed and his mouth slightly open, asked the man looking after him if he were dead. Before he could reply the patient said—" Me? I'm not going to die! I'm all right!" And he didn't die either, but went down the line with the others.

Accidents occurred in the Aid Post too. I remember a chap being wounded in the neck and carried to the Aid Post, where he was certified dead and put into the mortuary along with two or three other dead. He lay there all night, and next morning a burial party came up to bury these dead. They were proceeding to wrap the men in blankets preparatory to taking them to the graveyard when this man of whom I am writing rose up and enquired what was the matter. The men of the burial party were somewhat astonished, but one at least kept his head and explained that he had been wounded and was waiting his turn to go to the Aid Post. He was duly brought in and certified very much alive before being sent to the Field Ambulance.

Though there was much of sadness and suffering to be seen in an Aid Post, there was also some amusement. An Irish artilleryman was wounded in his leg on one occasion and caused rather a sensation by refusing to allow a stretcher-bearer near him, because, he declared "if anyone touches that leg it will drop off!" The stretcher-bearers once brought in a man who had been left on the road for dead for most of a day. They saw him moving, however, and fetched him in. He had been lying close to two men obviously killed, and it was thought that he must have been hit by a piece of the shell that accounted for these two men. When he came to the Aid Post a thorough search failed to locate any wound, and everyone, including the Medical Officer, was mystified until one of the men suggested "smelling his breath." This was tried and it was discovered that some "lot" had got a short rum ration that morning!

The onus of dressing and attending the wounded did not lie on the Medical Officer alone, but also on the men in the Aid Post. I remember on one occasion a man was brought in badly wounded in the shoulder, and with most of the flesh and part of the bone of the upper leg torn away—the result of a "dud" shell dropping on him. He was very anxious that the leg should be saved, but as this was impossible and as he was suspicious of the Medical Officer, one of the men was told to cut off the leg. The wound was too big to be painful, so that no chloroform was necessary. (We had chloroform, but the only use I saw it put to was to take stains out of the Medical Officer's tunic). The only lance that could cut was a small scalpel with a blade about one inch long! The man detailed for the job started to cut in the ordinary way, but without success, so he gripped the scalpel like a dagger and hacked at the limb till it came off. He got all the flesh cut, but when he came to the large sinews at the back of the leg they merely "twanged" like fiddle-strings and the wounded man made a most peculiar noise, as if he rather liked it. The sinews were cut with scissors, and the leg removed, The patient, however, died.

For the most part when the wounded men came to the Aid Post they tried, even when in great pain, to put a cheerful face on things. They raised a wry smile and a feeble joke, and, as they moved off towards the Field ambulances would inform the Aid Post men that they were "laughing sandbags," and would soon be in Blighty now! And if the man had got a "Cushy one," the Aid Post men would cordially agree among themselves that he was a "lucky beggar." For a wound that was "cushy" and looked like a "Blighty one" was all that a man desired in time of war.

XIV
"THE SPIRITS OF THE TROOPS ARE EXCELLENT!"
22ND MAY, 1920

I HAVE endeavoured to give my readers some idea of those daily sufferings and inconveniences that made up the life of the soldier, and I shall try in this article to present the sort of moral code which he was taught while in the Army so that one may have some idea of how a young impressionable lad could be assisted along the "primrose path that leadeth to the everlasting bonfire"; for it should be understood that, besides the physical discomforts, with their inevitable results, the soldier had much to endure morally which, in the ordinary course of a sheltered civilian life, he would not have had to face. I should first express the opinion—I do not ask my readers to agree if they do not think I am right—that men cannot live the lives of animals without losing something of their culture. The life of the soldier on active service was really the life of an animal. He was wrought at irregular hours and for long periods, he was herded with others, usually overcrowded, into holes in the earth, he was fed and watered—insufficiently in the summer-time usually—clothed and shod, looked after by officers and senior N.C.Os, and, especially, was "hunted," never knowing when he was to be wounded or killed, and therefore had to adopt the wariness of hunted animals and keep a keen watch on the movements of the hunters in the shape of "sentry-go." Added to this he had few opportunities of reading and little to read when he had the opportunity. He had his newspapers from home and his letters. The newspapers were full of the war, illustrated with photographs of heroes being decorated, wounded heroes, "our cheerful wounded," batches of German prisoners, and so on, all of which were of no interest to the soldier. He knew the price of victory and that was what a victory meant for him: so many pals "gone west," so many shifted to hospital, and he still there waiting his turn. He knew all about German prisoners and the neat way they had of keeping a machine-gun going and hacking gaps in troops till these troops were actually on the gun, when the hands would go up and the enemy cry "kamerade," and get sent down the line to be better fed than the poor unfortunates who had to guard them. He hated to see the phrase, so common in the newspapers, "The spirits of the troops are excellent!" The spirits of the troops were just like the spirits of other people. Monotony does not tend to make men cheerful, and it can therefore be taken for granted that the spirits of the troops were not excellent. After the first novelty of being in the war zone wore off, the men just got "fed up" and stayed " fed up." When they were leaving the trenches for a rest they felt less "fed up," and consequently more cheerful, but the depression settled again when the time came to resume duty in the line. The spirits of the troops were excellent only when they got leave, and the excellence of their spirits dropped considerably when they had to go back. The letters from home were usually more cheerful, but many wrote complaining and grumbling letters and so did much to keep the regiments in a low state of spirits. Because the soldiers kicked a ball with enthusiasm, or visited a canteen with celerity whenever possible and when they had money, or "poshed up" and set off for a stroll through a half-ruined town or city with a late pass, it was not because they were feeling particularly cheerful but because they were getting a change from the ceaseless monotony and because they were looking for the cheerfulness they seldom found.

But it was not of the spirits of the troops that I started to write, and so will get to my subject. Even when a soldier had money he did not always have the opportunity to spend it, so that the opportunist, who is always with us, found the means to part the soldier and his money, and at the same time give him a little excitement. In other words, all manner of card and other games on which money could be lost and won were always in evidence wherever there were a few soldiers gathered together. Of course it is illegal to gamble in the Army, but that fact was "blinked" when the troops crossed over the Channel, and I have even seen a "gambling school" concentrating on "Crown and Anchor"[5] in a little dug-out in the side of a trench round which German shells were falling, if not profusely, at least in uncomfortable numbers and proximity. When the soldiers were in a town where money could be spent there was one place where all were sure of a welcome, and that was at an estaminet, or the French equivalent to our public house. (I know that there was always a Y.M.C.A. but in nearly every place where there was an estaminet, and also probably a Church Army or other hut, these soon became crowded and any refreshments required—tea, etc.—had to be fetched from a counter to which there was always a lengthy queue, the result was that those soldiers who wanted company and found these places packed went to the only other available place—the estaminet). In the areas near the battle zone these estaminets were not run on the much vaunted "Continental style," but very much like the English or Scottish "pub", there being a limited number of seats and tables scattered round so the men could sit down in comfort and "yarn" over their drinks. Besides the desire for this company there was a natural curiosity to taste the foreign "drinks." To men who were used with spirits and beer and had a nodding acquaintance with port wine and sherry, the white and red wine served to them in a French or Belgian Estaminet, in the language of the soldier, "caught them bending." The white wine was the more expensive, and therefore became the favourite drink as being sure to be better than the red. I may mention that the wine supplied to soldiers was horrible stuff, immature and raw, and not the kind of thing a Frenchman would look at. The white wine could be bought by the bottle at a price that put it to the British purchaser on a level with beer, and like beer they drank it. They did not, like the Frenchman, sit the long night through sipping their wine and smoking and playing cards; they filled up a glass and swallowed it off with a "Cheerio!" and filled it up again. So it was not a case of spending the night over a bottle of wine but a case of getting rid of as much wine as the time would allow! The natural results followed. White wine, even bad white wine, was not beer, as the soldiers who had participated could avow next morning. And so the soldier, for want of a little friendly warning and education in the matter of drinks, got the taste for drinking, with its one gift of forgetfulness, which often compensated for the sore heads and dry mouths of the following morning and the nights spent in the Guard Room!

---

5   Denis Winter: "The only game for the gambling hard-core was Crown and Anchor. Illegal at the time, it is hard today to find out the rules, though a pub near the Elephant and Castle in South London keeps the name alive. The board for the game was divided into six sections – spades, diamonds, clubs, hearts, crown and anchor. There were three dice with a symbol of the game on each facet. The participant placed his money on one of the board symbols. If that figure came up on all three dice, the man got three times his stake back, if on two, double, and so on. In the parlance of the game, the crown was the sergeant-major, the spade the shovel, the diamond the curse and the anchor the meathook. The game might be known as bumble and Buck, and the symbols as the dart (heart), shamrock (club), gravedigger (spade) and Kimberley (diamond).

42

It frequently happened that the soldier lost some part of his kit. When that happened, unless he lost it "under shell fire," the renewal was entered in his paybook for reduction off his pay. That being the case, it naturally followed that the men objected to paying for things lost, especially when they were not always in a position to keep a strict eye on their property. So they would go to their platoon sergeant or some one else likely to know these things, and enquire as to what they lost, and invariably they got the answer—"You know what you do: find it"—which, being interpreted meant replace the article at the expense of someone else's kit. And if the man was too honest to do that, he had to pay for the article, and probably found that, for his honesty, someone had "won" something from his kit, which generally had the effect of curing his honesty! Looting, of course, was forbidden, but few German prisoners got far down the line with anything in their pockets save crumbs, while French houses left hurriedly by their occupants were well searched for anything of a convenient size worth carrying off. The fact is—again this is my opinion—after a brief stay in the Army "over there," men got an altogether false idea of the value of money and a wrong conception of property rights. The earth was the Lord's and all that was in it, and as fighting soldiers to a good cause whatever they came across worthy of taking and of convenient carrying capacity they took. It requires the exercise of a great deal of caution and will-power to break from habits so easily formed, and men who have faced death and fought hard for their lives are not the men either to exercise caution or to turn their will-power to the breaking of habits which add a certain zest to life. Men must be educated out of bad habits and into proper lines of action, and no one, so far as I know, has taken the trouble or had the ability to devise a means of eradicating the lowering influences of the war on those who took part in it.

I have not, by any means exhausted this subject, nor have I shown to any great degree how much damage was done, as the direct result of the war, to the moral side of the men, who, initially, at any rate, were prepared to sacrifice all for a cause, but I think—I hope—I have said enough to make those who were sheltered from its blighting influences "gently scan their brother man," and remember that those men gave the best years of their lives to fight for freedom, and collected their weaknesses in the process.

XV
A DECIDED LACK OF RELIGION IN THE ARMY
5TH JUNE, 1920

THE FOLLOWING article may prove of some interest, though it does not perhaps have any vital bearing on what was meant by doing one's bit. The subject I wish to take up is one that has been much ventilated both in the press and in books on the war, and by much abler pens than mine; but perhaps my views on the subject may call the attention of my readers to a fact which is somewhat glossed over at the present time—the failure of the Church to have a proper contact with the vast majority of the people of this country; for the subject I am dealing with is the soldiers and Christianity. Now, when one speaks of soldiers, one is really speaking of the young manhood of the country, for it was these men, drawn from civilian life, who made up the Army which helped to beat the Germans and brought about a great victory which has, through the short-sighted policy of the peace makers, left us wondering whether we actually did win the war, or merely brought it to an end, with its glorious train of Empires and Nations bound together in a cause, to replace with the pathetic picture of a world as it is today. So that, to speak of the soldier and religion, is to speak of the mass of British manhood and their outlook on religion. Needless to say, I can only speak of the men among whom I lived, but these changed continually through the wastage of war, so that I actually met a very great number, and could not necessarily but notice the sort of lives they lived and can judge from that their attitude towards religion with tolerable accuracy. And in giving the matter consideration the main outstanding feature seems to me to be that the Church, the teacher of religion and the stimulator of religious fervour, has almost entirely lost touch with the manhood of the country; and what little foundation on which to build up some structure of religious thought the men had carried away from civilian life, the Army, with its drum-head services and its Church parades, its bestial conditions of life and its retrograde environment, did its best to destroy.

I do not mean to suggest that the men I met were bad or that all were irreligious. Far from it. I have actually met two or three men who were highly religious. I met several theological students—Welshmen—who were in the R.A.M.C., and who were wont to conduct services in the Y.M.C.A. hut in the camp in which they trained. That was on this side of the Channel. I also met a man in an infantry camp who read from his Bible each day and knelt beside his "bed" each night and said his prayers. (I may add, for the benefit of those who may think that the other men present scoffed at him, that this soldier was held in the highest respect by the men of his hut, who admired him, not so much for being religious, but because of the fact that he had the courage of his convictions). In France I met one man—a corporal—who was really religious and who was said to be a lay preacher. He was a "good sort," and used to be very gravely censorious when he heard a man swearing. The vehement repetition of lurid language was the stock conversation of most soldiers in times of stress—personal or otherwise—so that the corporal never had long waits between his droppings of the good seed. He was finally very badly hit, and died on his journey to the Aid Post, and the last words I heard him say as he left the line, and probably the last words he uttered, were:-"Oh Lord, why hast Thou forsaken me?", which he repeated several times in a loud voice. I was sitting beside a western Highlander at the time, a young lad and a grocer's assistant in civilian life. He was not by any means religious, and after cogitating for some time after the wounded man was removed he turned to me and solemnly said: "That's an awful thing for a Christian to say when he's hit!" or words to that effect.

It is never, of course, safe to judge as to what really constitutes religion to any single individual; which is another way of saying that the Church has failed to carry out its obligations to teach Christianity to the people. I remember a soldier, three times wounded, who said to me, quite solemnly, that he knew he was not a good chap and was an awful swearer, "but," he added, "every time I go over the top I pray like hell to come back safe again!" In the Battalion in which I served during the hostilities there was a young lad who had joined up when he had recently passed his matriculation examination. His father was a minister and his uncle also was in the ministry. He himself was a good lad and meant to follow in his father's footsteps. He was killed. One of his two friends, a young plumber, was very much cut up about his death—his other pal had been badly wounded—and, speaking of it, said that that chap should not have been killed, because surely he had been well prayed for! He meant to convey, I presume, that his belief in the efficacy of prayer had had a nasty jar; which is another demonstration of the fact that the Church cannot be working on the proper lines actually to touch the young men of the nation.

As everyone knows the Government did their best to see that the spiritual needs of the troops were provided for. Each unit had its "padre," and some of them were all right and some were not. As a class my own opinion is that the Catholic "padres" took far more interest in the individual men in their care than did any other of the spiritual guides, and I should think, from my observations, that more decorations were won by Catholic priests in proportion to their number than by the "padres" of the other creeds and sects. No doubt this personal interest in each Catholic was fostered by the confessional, when the "padre" came into close contact with each man, finding out his weaknesses and desiring to help him in his hours of stress, besides the onus on the priest to give communion to each man before he "passed out."

I mentioned Church parades and drum-head services. When one joined the Army one had to state one's religion, and so far as I am aware none of the men admitted having no religion at all. I knew one man who gained for himself a large amount of respect for his astuteness and no little envy in designating himself a spiritualist. He refused to be cajoled into believing that he was really Church of England or Presbyterian, and the result was that he did not have any Church parade at all! On this side of the Channel Church parade was a very solemn affair. The men of each denomination were drawn up, polished and shining, inspected and marched off to a central parade ground where they were again inspected before being marched, headed by a band, to the Church, where they heartily sang the hymns, dozed through the prayers, paid little or no attention to the sermon and were heartily glad when it was all over. Much of the Sunday morning was spent in far from prayerful language because of the necessity of having to "posh up" to go to Church! Had the men been left to go or not to go to Church of their own free will, and without having to undergo the ordeal of an inspection, I have no doubt that many would have turned out, if not for any other reason, just for the sake of the walk to Church, but to be forced to go, and with the chance of being "pulled" because of a lack of gloss on the edges of one button or for some such ridiculous offence, did not encourage the soldier to take kindly to religion and certainly did not help to bring him into closer touch with his "padre." In France and Belgium the parade was supposed to be a drum-head service, and many an impressive picture have I seen of these services in the recent war. Usually the pictures showed a group of devout soldiers gathered round an earnest "padre" with the drum prominently placed in the picture. Personally I never saw a drum at these services. We just had an ordinary Church parade, but were preached to in the open instead of in a building. The services were usually short, the singing hearty, the sermon brief and easily forgotten. The men cursed as they "poshed" up for the occasion, and were glad when the parade was over. Had it been left to the men themselves few would have turned out, most of them preferring a long rest in such billets as they occupied. The Church parade as a means of bringing religion to the soldier was in his own language a "wash out." I do not think that the fact of his being an officer did anything to make a "padre" unpopular with his men, nor did the fact that he was the "padre" make him less liked. Out of respect for him—I do not think it was what he asked for—the men might have been less lurid in their conservation when he was obviously about, but if he was manly he was spoken well of as being "a decent old sport," or "not half a bad chap for a padre." If he was not manly (and some forgot they were men and only remembered they were ministers) the men were quick to see it and thought so much the less of him. There was, I should say, a decided lack of religion in the Army, and therefore among the male portion of the nation as a whole, though there was plenty of belief in Christianity, and certainly a great deal of its practice, unconscious practice perhaps, which might have been utilised to bring men into closer touch with the Churches, but which, by wrong methods, was not so utilised. There can be no doubt but that the Churches missed a great opportunity during the war, and nothing but a revolution in the methods of teaching can, I am convinced, get the people and the Church into proper contact again.

XVI
THE GREAT RETREAT, MARCH 1918
19TH JUNE, 1920

I PURPOSE now to deal with my experiences in the great retreat of March, 1918. As I said, these experiences do not represent a history of the war, and this will not read like any official account of what took place, so that any opinions I express are purely personal and cannot claim the weight or accuracy of the account as supplied to Headquarters of the commander of our Brigade for instance. Our Battalion was on the Roeux front, across the canal, at the commencement of the retreat on this, the Arras front, but prior to that we were comfortably ensconced in a fine trench on the safe side of the water, and we were enjoying splendid weather. As we were actually awaiting the attack we had no fatigues except to fetch up rations, and our only discomfort was the chill of the night when we took our round of sentry-go. During the day we lolled about, basking ourselves in the sun and watching for any movement on the "other side." Needless to say we, the rank and file, had no idea that an attack was pending, and we were quite content to take our share of sunshine and idleness without questioning the wherefore of our lack of fatigues. We were, indeed, very comfortable, and there was no shell fire from either side. There was an occasional bark from a machine gun and there was a sniper who harassed us a little, but an artillery observation officer "spotted" one fine afternoon and he "ceased from troubling." We spent a few days in this delightful fashion and then we were moved across the canal.

The trench system across the canal was all right, and our duties were as light there as they had been before. We were put into the "caves," large underground chalk-pits, fitted with water tanks and electric lights, and here we rested day and night, only taking our turn at guard. I remember that, the first day we were in the caves, most of us made a rush to get a wash and a shave, for even a few days without either, despite the fine weather, left one very grimy. It should be understood that a soldier actually in the line is not allowed to remove his equipment. Well, our company commander (who, of course, was quite aware of the impending attack), happened to stroll through the cave at this particular moment, and he had tears in his voice, and I have no doubt tears in his eyes, when he lectured our platoon sergeant, who was sleeping peacefully under his great-coat, at his remissness in allowing his men to doff not only their equipment but also their tunics, and, in one or two instances, even their shirts, to indulge in the luxury of a shave and a wash! However, his lecture came too late for most of us, for, having begun, we did not cease until our ablutions were complete. The front line of this system was not "held" in the usual sense, but each evening a section was told off to patrol the trench all night and given Verey lights or flares to set off should "Jerry" show any signs of activity. I was on this patrol three nights running, but I rather enjoyed it as we got a corner to ourselves with instructions that we were not to be disturbed during the day! Also the sergeant in charge was not at all an excitable individual, and he put us "two on" at a time, giving the other four their usual four hours sleep and two hours sentry go, thus allowing us our usual nights' rest as well as our restful day. We were having, in fact, a "posh" time and were really glad of it. On the fourth night I was not on the front line patrol, and it was on the morning of the fifth day that the Germans "came over." On the day before he came over, however, we had a little bit of excitement. A party of Germans came across to give us a present of a few bombs. One was thrown into our trench—the front line was unmanned at the time—but it burst harmlessly away from anybody, and the man who was going to throw the second had a mishap, the bomb going off before he got rid of it with the result that he blew lumps off himself and the others "skinned out" with their casualty. A party of our boys, with a couple of bombs each, gave chase, but they did not get their quarry and returned with their bombs intact.

On the morning of our fifth day "in" we had an unusually early call to "stand to," and arrived from the safety of the cave to be greeted with a hefty barrage which lasted eleven hours and caused us quite a number of casualties. It was only now that I began to grasp the meaning of our days of ease, as I wondered whether I was going to get a "cushy Blighty one" or something bigger, and kept wondering these long eleven hours as the shells showered down and the casualties walked, staggered, or were carried to the Regimental Aid Post—that is those casualties that did not lie where they fell, to await such burial as soldiers on active service get. Finally, the Germans came over themselves. They came on our left, and crossed the skyline at about right angles to the part of the trench our platoon occupied, so that our Lewis gun crew accounted for quite a number as they went. We of course, did not know exactly what was happening on the left, but quite suddenly we got orders to retreat. Glad to move, we got under way and made for the cave entrance, for our line of retreat lay through the cave into another trench. I got rather a shock when making down the trench to see that only a few yards divided our last man and the first of the Germans, who was cautiously advancing down the trench, taking advantage of the corners as he came. Someone "handed" him a bomb and stopped his career. The entrance to the cave was narrow and the men got rather crowded at the door, which, by the way, was to be blown up when the last man passed through. The Germans were close upon us, however, before we could all get inside the door, and a man with a revolver, one of the Lewis gun crew, stepped out of the mass, and emptied his weapon into the advancing enemy, causing them to come to a halt, and allowing the rest of our men to pass through. One of the Germans tried to throw a bomb, but the bomb must have been bad, for this also burst in his hand, though I did not wait to see what damage was done. The hero of the revolver had hardly passed through the door when it was blown up and he was thrown down the steps to the bottom of the cave. We hurried through and came to the next trench, took up our positions and once more came under the hail of the enemy's shells. He had the range to a nicety, and added considerably to our casualties by the accuracy of his fire. There were two things that struck me here. One thing was that our artillery seemed to be singularly silent and I drew the inference that it had "pulled out" and was "well away," and felt very bitter that the infantry should be left thus unsupported to stem an attack by what was obviously superior numbers, backed by an energetic and accurate artillery. The other thing I noticed was that our "superiority in the air" had seemingly received a nasty jar, for I only saw— on the small bit of front in which I was interested, of course—two British aeroplanes to about a dozen or more Boche. The German airmen were very daring, and skimmed our trenches at no great height above the parapet and in a leisurely fashion, enfilading us with their machine gun fire. It was very aggravating to stand there helpless, with hundredweights of iron and steel flying all round one, while an airman pumped bullets into the trench. We fired at the planes, but either our fire was ineffectual or the body of the machine was armour-plated, for our fire had no effect. If the German airmen were daring, our two pilots were doubly so. They dashed in at great speed, took what observations they wanted, and dashed back again, right through the German aeroplanes, firing into them as they went. Their work passes description. All the time they were outnumbered, yet they always came through. I saw one hemmed in by four enemy aeroplanes, and, to the eyes of the infantry, cornered, but suddenly he dashed down till he almost skimmed the ground, and then rose gradually in his speedy return to the British line. These aeroplanes, were, I imagine, observing for our artillery, though as far as I could see we did not have a great mass of artillery to whom to report.

XVII
THE GERMANS FAIL TO SECURE THE VICTORY
26TH JUNE, 1920

THE TRENCH which we were holding was a wide, comfortable trench, revetted with "basketwork," and with the fine weather very dry. The little dug-outs were lined with wood and altogether it might have been one of those "show" trenches which were leisurely dug and which had a lot of time spent on their improvement back in Blighty. It was the sort of trench one dreamed of but seldom saw, though just at this particular moment it was not the most pleasant place to make a long stand. Its width rather diminished its utility as a protection, for many shells actually burst in the walls of the trench causing much havoc, and it soon became untenable. We held this splendid piece of workmanship about one quarter of an hour, and up to that time I at least had never come across a trench of anything like its desirability, nor did I ever again run across another quite like it. It was just our luck to see such a trench, hold it under difficulties for a quarter of an hour, and then never see it again! To leave this trench meant crossing the canal, which was an operation none of us were anxious to carry out. However, the order came, and we hurried off. The trench "angled" sharply to the canal, and that piece of it was anything but cheerful. It had been hammered out of all recognition by direct hits, and there were a lot of dead and a few wounded lying in it, covered with dirt and some practically buried. We took with us what wounded we could and hurried on, but not a few "stopped a bit," as they passed through. Finally we got to the open ground and raced for the bridge over the canal.

Strange to say only a few stray shells fell on this open ground, which was below an embankment and thus out of the range of machine-gun fire, so that we did not have any casualties here. The railway bridge across the canal had been blown up previously, and the "bridge" we had to cross was one of wooden planking built under the shelter of the damaged structure. The bridge was narrow and set on wooden props, so that it threatened to throw us off at practically every step. Most of us got across all right, but I saw a very tall soldier and a shorter one carry a wounded Captain across on an improvised stretcher. When the bridge began to "jump," the men naturally tried to steady themselves, the final result of their contortions being that they threw the casualty into the water and held up the retreat while they fished him out again. We now began to retreat in earnest, and flew along, shedding kit as we went. Our machine-gunners were doing splendid work here. With no infantry between them and the enemy they sat on, firing merrily away, and, though I naturally did not stop to examine the results, they must have caused the Higher Command some anxiety when they scanned the lists of their disabled cannon fodder.

We were not greatly troubled in our run back, although an occasional bit of "heavy stuff" fell in uncomfortable proximity, and one had a little more time to look round. I saw a great pal of mine a short distance ahead and hurried to him to get his views on the matter. Actually, I may say, though most of us were of opinion that we were on the way to defeat—we knew not of the plans of our General Staff—the men were quite cheerful and exhilerated. My friend greeted me with a smile and the remark that "the spirits of the troops were excellent," adding that he was feeling quite hungry but had come away in such a hurry that he had inadvertently left his rations. I had my "pound of bread" intact, so we went on, each with a swiftly disappearing slice of bread and marmalade in his hand. Finally we came to our supports and found a most forlorn band of Englishmen sitting in the wreck of a trench about which the German heavy artillery was dropping shells in profusion. The dead were scattered round everywhere. I saw one of our officers sit down in this trench, calmly light a cigarette and fall to studying a map. Not a yard from where he sat lay a man with both his legs off at the knee, while another lay stretched across him with a huge gash in his back. We did not rest long in this trench but passed on leaving the supports to follow after when they felt that the locality was unhealthy enough. We went a good distance further over the open but were lucky in having no casualties. I may say that we did not pass any other troops, so that I think from what I saw and without any knowledge of what they were having to face, that, had the Germans pushed on, they could have broken through and gone where they wanted.

Our retreat finally came to an end at an old uncared for trench below an embankment upon which stood a battery of French heavy guns monotonously barking every minute or so. Here we were very unfortunate, and I personally had three large sized shocks. First, as we stepped into the trench to "dig ourselves in," for the trench as it was offered no protection. I was looking round for a likely spot at which to start. As I looked a shell burst in the trench at some distance from where I stood and right on a man who was also looking for a spot at which to commence digging. When the smoke cleared away that soldier had entirely disappeared. The second shock was when a heavy shell fell close to several men and gave us seven casualties, including two officers, one of whom had one leg blown off and the other his left arm shattered. One of the men was literally torn to pieces, his kilt being blown across the wire and part of him being left in the trench. To see seven healthy men being thus reduced to six serious casualties and one corpse did give us a nauseous sensation. The next shock I got was more personal. My pal and I, who were digging together, stood up to exchange some remark when we heard the spiteful hiss of a shell falling close. We both ducked but my pal was killed, part of his head being blown off. This bit of skull struck me a violent blow on the chest, while the violence of the explosion threw me to the ground. When I picked myself up I was very badly shaken, not so much the result of being knocked about as from the shock I had received, and I really had not the physical strength left to continue digging. The shells continued to fall, but for some reason the range had been lengthened and our trench was left in peace.

That evening it began to rain, and late at night, though we were all heartily tired and anxious for a rest, we were ordered to move off to another trench where we spent several days in comparative quietness. Then we moved to some gunpits, where again we had a tolerably quiet time. At the time of the retreat we got no rations on two nights and had to do with very little food, but then we got extra rations, including cooked meat, and lots of extras like tinned cocoa and milk and cafe au lait. We had a royal time there, but like all royal times it soon finished and we were transferred to a waterlogged trench tenanted by an army of frogs where we spent some three or four miserable days sopping wet from the knees down. After we were transferred to dug-outs in a railway embankment, where we indulged in a much needed wash and shave and general clean up prior to going out on a well-earned and much longed for rest. This rest was the first solid evidence we had that the retreat was over and that the Germans had failed to secure the victory, which most of us thought had lain in their grasp.

Our time of trial was not over, however. We were one day hurried off in motors, and by train to an unknown destination which we ultimately discovered was La Bassée Canal, where the Germans had broken through the Portuguese troops. I saw in an official account that the Portuguese had made a gallant stand. Perhaps they did, I do not know, as our division were not the first British troops on the spot. The 51st Division were the first reinforcements, and a gallant stand they made. They had nothing good to say of the Portuguese troops—that is, those with whom I spoke.

This Division, outnumbered and caught unawares in the open, fought a tremendous fight and, despite losing a vast number of their soldiers, held the Germans and stemmed the attack until the arrival of the 55th Division—which also did very fine work. When we arrived, therefore, there was little for me to do but consolidate the position which was comparatively easy as the Germans had been driven across the Canal. We were agreeably surprised at our good fortune, for prior to our arrival in the fighting area we had been met by refugees by the dozen and motor loads of casualties, and naturally expected that we were in for a "rough time." That came in due course, but at first we had a "cushy" time in a trench system which was passably dry in fine weather. I may add that the Portuguese were never again in the line, but were employed constructing trenches.

XVIII
"A LAND FLOWING WITH MILK AND HONEY"
2ND JULY, 1920

AFTER settling at La Bassée Canal we had a brief period of restful occupation in fine weather in a country only recently evacuated by its inhabitants. The character of the landscape was entirely different to that to which we had been used, instead of the barrenness of bleak, shell-swept country on which there was nothing green, where every tree was battered out of all recognition, the stumps standing up like badly damaged teeth, where the villages that once stood around were only to be found by a careful study of a map of the district or from the signs which stood on other sites and boldly proclaimed that this was such and such a place, where every yard of the earth's surface was pitted with shell-holes, we were dwelling on land that pictured beautifully the peace of which one reads. The villages stood very much as usual, though practically every house had received some damage from shell-fire, but in the distance, at least, each hamlet looked as it had done a few weeks before, the centre of a rich-yielding agricultural countryside. It was a great change compared with the place we had left, where every house had been shattered by the devastating shell-fire and every village and hamlet had been reduced to what cannot be better described than by the Shetland word "bruck." At our new sector the trees were flourishing, the orderly fields were a testimony to the industry of the people who had recently left them, and the animals on the farm—cattle, goats, pigs, ducks and poultry—roamed around at will; scared, no doubt, by the sounds of the guns and by their unnatural freedom. Needless to say the soldiers made the most of this wonderful country, "a land flowing with milk and honey." There were potatoes, a luxury the taste of which we had almost forgotten, and all sorts of vegetables. There were also eggs and milk, for the Battalion in which I was a unit was a north-country one, and contained many farm servants, and, these men could milk cows and did so with zest; there were also fresh meat and fowls, because the boys did not scruple to slay a hen or two—strictly against regulations—for a succulent dinner, nor were they averse to killing a cow or a pig for the sake of a piece of steak or a rasher of fresh pork. Of course, these cattle, etc., did not remain there long, as soldiers were sent up from "behind" to collect and drive them out of gun range, but before that happened many had met a violent death at the hands of the enemy, and not a few at the hands of our Division. It is the soldiers' prerogative to "scrounge," to look round for what he can find, and it was not many hours after our arrival on this sector till our "scroungers" discovered a very important thing, that the inhabitants in their flight, had left their cellars well stocked with wine and beer. In the fine days that followed the consolidation of our trench it was no unusual thing to find a "Tommy" quaffing champagne from a bottle, or "downing" all sorts of wines with gusto, while in the evenings between watches, a rush would be made to the nearer houses and each man would take turns at the tap of a beer barrel and fill his "canteen" to "wet his whistle" when he took his stand on the fire step for his "two hours on"—all of which, of course, constituted grave crimes in the Army and could be visited with serious punishments. That, however; did not deter the men to any great extent, and though these breaches of regulations lasted as long as did the wine and beer, I never heard of any one being "pulled" for it. It is needless to add that the liquors did not last long, for a Division of troops can make a big hole in anything of a gastronomic nature in an amazingly brief period.

In a very short time the face of the countryside changed. Soon the German guns got the range and pumped shells ceaselessly all around, so that the trees began to get smashed, the green fields were torn up and the houses were gradually reduced to broken bricks and tiles scattered about, while the roads, always the target of the artillery, soon became a series of shell holes linked up with bits of damaged road. We were wont to go back from the line to a small hamlet, not out of heavy gun range but safe for all practical purposes, and every night while we were there German aeroplanes came over and "dropped a few," so that during the period we were there, some five or six months, we were never out of intimate danger and never had a really sound night's rest.

Besides this occasional shell fire and bomb dropping, the Germans used to send over large quantities of gas and gas shells, which added to the general misery of our existence in that sector. We had not held our position on the bank of the Canal long before we got orders to go forward and reconnoitre, with the result that we established two posts across the Canal, one small post held by one's platoon, and a trench which was held by a company. The land was water-logged, so that one could only dig down some three to three and a half feet, and the residue of the protection had to be thrown up in the form of parapets. The ground smelled evilly, owing, I am told, to the great quantities of artificial manure used by the natives, so that it was not good to stand in a trench, especially on a hot day, when the moist earth steamed and the smell from the earth seemed to be accentuated. In April the Germans "came over"[6] again on this sector. I was at the time in the forward post and was actually on sentry, but really I was dozing comfortably when I got a severe dig and was told to "skin out." Naturally, I wanted to know what was the matter, but was told to hurry and make no noise. I collected my "impedimenta" and hurried. We went through the company post and across the Canal to our original trench. The daylight had not made its appearance, so that I could see nothing, but my

---

[6]   On the 13th – 15th April, 1918, the 2nd Seaforths were part of I Corps, First Army, and took part in the Battle of Hazebrouck, including the defence of Hinges Ridge, and the Battle of Bethune.

"doze" must have been a fairly substantial one, as I was informed here that the barrage—and it was no mean one—had been going on for over an hour, and I only noticed it when I "settled" on the far side of the Canal. Strange to say, there were no shells falling near to our trench, but further back the trenches were getting a terrible trouncing, and still further back there was a great deal of havoc wrought. It was rather anomalous that the front line troops, who were supposed to bear the brunt of the attack, and consequently suffer most heavily, got off with extremely few casualties, while the Battalion Headquarters, which were well back of the line, had a large number of casualties, and troops holding support lines came in for a severe trouncing! With the coming of daylight we saw the Germans. Our company post retired to our side of the Canal, after doing some fine work, and we set to and fired steadily into the advancing enemy. He had a lot of shelter from two woods, but his casualties were very heavy, and our artillery was very effective. Some of our boys (a patrol) were left across the Canal, and they came to the edge of the stream, closely followed by the Germans, only to discover that the bridge had been blown up. They got into a boat, without oars, and started to paddle across with bits of wood, but came under a hail of machine gun bullets, and the officer in charge was killed. The boat landed all right, however, and these lads, who were practically prisoners, managed to reach our line. Among these men was a Lerwegian. So close had they been to the enemy in their run for our lines that one of the party was taken prisoner. Another, who was wounded in the ankle, managed to drag himself along the edge of the Canal and took shelter in a sunk barge till night, when he was brought across. The Germans had planned their attack well, and one party got across a pontoon bridge and started to come over. A sergeant got up on to the embankment in full view of the enemy, and smashed away at the Huns with hand grenades to such good purpose that some fifty rushed in and gave themselves up as prisoners, while the others retreated and cast off the bridge. The attack was a complete failure, and, according to a report in the London *Times*, one of the most costly to the Germans. During the attack, when the effort to cross the Canal had failed, and the enemy saw that there was no hope, the men made for what shelter they could. Three men ran into a house close to the Canal bank, but hardly had they arrived than a trench mortar shell went in the roof. Almost immediately after the Germans waved a sheet out of one of the windows and shouted "Kamerade!" However, before this could be communicated to the trench mortar crew another shell "arrived," to be greeted with a wild fluttering of the sheet, which did not avail, however, for a third burst into the house. This was too much for one of the men, and he darted outside and into a shell-hole. Just as he landed so did a trench mortar shell and the German sailed gracefully out of the hole, and "the subsequent proceedings interested him no more." During the day our artillery kept up a brisk fire, and added considerably to the enemy casualties, while several Germans, in an endeavour to get to more substantial shelter than that afforded by a shell-hole, exposed themselves long enough for a rifle to prove an effective deterrent. Two of our lads had a competition that day in the "bagging of Jerries," and counted their "bag." They took that each German that fell and did not rise again was a casualty. I can't remember their exact figures, but I do remember their day's shooting was an excellent one from their point of view. If our artillery was brisk during the day they opened out in good earnest at night and their thorough "search" of the ground was very effective, as we in the front line knew from the shouts of the wounded and the cries of "Kamerade," to which, because of the water between us, we could not pay much attention. I believe that the casualties were so heavy and so "massed" that our aeroplanes went over the following day to get photographs of the heaps of dead. We felt very proud of our work here for we had stopped an attack in a very brief space of ground and in a very brief space of time, with the loss of about 100 yards of ground, when we were outnumbered, though, of course, we did not forget that, but for the Canal, things might have been much different. However, everybody was satisfied, except, I presume, the Germans, and this was the last occasion on which we had to face an actual attack by our enemy, though, of course, at that time we knew not, nor did we imagine, that the end of the war was so near at hand.

XIX
BLOODLESS AFFAIRS AND STUBBORN RESISTANCE
10TH JULY, 1920

WE WERE for some little time at La Bassée Canal, and had but a few really exciting moments during that time. As in the case of our arrival there, after the attack to which I referred to in the last article, we went gingerly forward, "feeling" for the enemy, occupying shell holes which we strengthened at each advance. These "advances" were bloodless affairs, carried out at night and meant the occupying of a few yards of ground across the Canal. Finally, we got to within a few hundred yards of the enemy and settled down. A few hundred yards may seem a considerable distance from an enemy, but it should be remembered that the country was flat with only hedges to block the view of anything approaching, and also that at that particular time we were acting on the defensive, and expected the enemy "over" any day, so the distance between the lines was all to our advantage, allowing us, as it did, an opportunity of getting in a lot of concentrated fire on an advancing mob, coming over flat and comparatively open country towards us in the shelter of our trenches. As I said, we "settled" and proceeded to link up the shell-holes we occupied, making a trench. Behind that, and between the first line and the Canal, we dug another trench, fitted up with barbed wire, etc., and generally had a busy, if non-exciting time. During this period the Germans attempted one raid on us. Under cover of darkness they collected in two large farm houses about fifty yards from our front line, and so in the "dawning light" debouched from there in mass as usual. They were "spotted" at once, and our machine guns, Lewis guns and rifles opened out, so that the Huns did not attempt to come further, but retired precipitately, leaving a goodly number of casualties behind. We tried several raids in this sector, two of which were ghastly failures, one or two met with indifferent success—we came out no better than the enemy—and one was a splendid success. On the whole, however, we were very quiet and more or less bored.

I remember two incidents which occurred here that are rather worthy of note. For a time the German artillery used to send over gas shells every day, mostly mustard gas, and this naturally caused us great inconvenience. Incidentally it spoiled the water supply of the district, and one day caught almost an entire company of ours unawares, with the result that practically all of them had to go to hospital. This left us short-handed, and with plenty of fatigues to do, left us exceedingly wrathful. Inspiration came to someone in the Higher Command and it was decided to give the Germans a little gas in return. A very large quantity was collected and sent over to the enemy artillery. The explosion as it was sent over was terrific, and the German artillery, probably fearing an attack, "let loose" a barrage. This ceased abruptly, however, and we learned of the efficacy of the British gas from the fact that for two whole days following this not a shell came over our way from the other side! There was a small copse between us and the enemy, and it was decided that this had better be removed. In the night the Engineers put several cylinders of oil among the trees and prepared them so that the pressure of a button would burst the cylinders, ignite the oil, which would, of course, destroy the obstacle in our observation. It was arranged to carry the plan into effect next morning after "stand down," and we in the line—who were, of course, quite unaware of what was going to take place—were rudely disturbed in the act of making our breakfast by a huge explosion. Every man jumped up to see what was "on," but all that was to be seen was a huge pall of smoke rising from the little wood. The smoke rose and cleared away, but the copse looked none the worse, and in fact, except for the incidental damage caused by shell fire, so stood till the time we left the sector.

Farther back were two large woods occupied by the enemy, and these, being really the only good bases for attacking purposes, were naturally marked out for capture. The woods were attacked on different days, and the attacks were confined to one Battalion on each occasion. The barrage in each case was bright and brief, the attack swift, though the resistance was fairly stubborn, and the result favourable to our arms. We captured a good few Germans here, among them being several very young lads, and several obviously not of A1 category. These woods after their capture came in for much shell-fire, but our trenches ran, not through the wood, but along one side and in front, so that the German artillery threw away a large quantity of munitions to no good purpose. After the seizure of these woods we settled down to the usual routine of fatigues, gas, air raids, desultory fire and boredom, which lasted until the great British offensive which concluded the hostilities by arms commenced. In front of one of the woods and a short distance from our trench, there was a heap of dead, composed of Germans and British, and numbering some 15 to 18. They lay there all the time we were there, as we could not get at them to bury them, for a German machine gun played over them continually. In the summer time these were not pleasant companions, and did not help one to enjoy one's food. Still we even got used to them, and all that pertained to them, not even objecting seriously to the flies which flew from them and settled on our rations! So far as this sector was concerned that great epoch making attack began in a very quiet and unobtrusive manner. Our aeroplanes saw the Germans preparing to retire and we were ordered to follow up and keep in touch with the enemy. Patrols were sent out and went after the retiring Huns in open formation. Their progress was necessary slow, but they kept the enemy well within fire. The German heavy artillery was drawn out, stopping occasionally on the road to "send over a few." The light artillery was ready for drawing out, and the preparations for the retiral were very complete, as our men found scarcely anything left on the ground over which they were advancing. The German main body was protected by posts consisting of one or two machine guns, manned by fairly large crews, and these caused our patrols a lot of bother, inflicting comparatively heavy casualties among our lads. We continued to follow the Germans until they prepared to make a stand, when our soldiers also "dug in" and waited developments.

While one of our patrols, a Lewis gun crew, were advancing, they were suddenly confronted with a couple of machine guns protruding from the windows of a farmhouse. Though taken completely unawares, the men acted with great coolness. They made ready their gun, fixed their bayonets, and made all the preparations for a charge. This warlike appearance disconcerted the German post and, without firing a shot at the seven men, they surrendered with their guns and ammunition. There were about 80 Germans, and they marched back to our lines carrying their machine guns with them, in charge of two of our boys. In that Lewis gun crew were, if I remember aright, two Shetlanders, one from Lerwick and one from Sandwick[7], the latter, I believe, being in charge of the section.

He was subsequently wounded, as also was the Lerwick man, later in continuance of the same attack, but in another sector.

---

[7] The Lewis Gunner from Sandwick may well have been James Nicolson of the 2nd Seaforths, who was wounded at La Bassée on 22nd April, 1918.

XX
OVER THE TOP WITH THE CANADIANS
17TH JULY, 1920

WHEN we left La Bassée Canal finally, it was to go "over the top" with Canadian troops[8] in Artois. We did not actually go over with them, but followed them up and reinforced them, when their lines became somewhat thinned. The platoon to which I belonged was rather unfortunate. We left in the night to take up our positions, and we somehow got lost, with the result that we tramped about all night looking for our Battalion. We were carrying all the necessaries a soldier carries when going into an attack, and the result was that when we at length reached our lines—somewhere in the later morning for we followed the Canadians after they had begun the attack, before the daylight came in—we were very tired and scarcely able for so arduous a job as attacking a stubborn enemy. While we were tramping around, because we had no idea in what direction our Battalion had gone, we came upon some of the Canadians lying in a sunken road having a brief rest before advancing to their "moving off" position. Just as we came among them Fritz loosed off about a dozen "heavies," and they landed right into a Canadian company lumped together and spread out anyhow. Almost the whole company were made casualties, and we (the lost platoon) had to assist in "clearing" the wounded. This we did by rough dressing them and putting them into dugouts close by, of which fact we informed an artillery observation officer who, no doubt, in due course got the word through to some Field Ambulance. How long the wounded had to lie untended, however, I do not know, but I should expect their evacuation would not have been too swift. After that we came across some tanks and later stumbled upon a dug-out which seemed to be connected with nothing in particular, and which was being fitted up as an aid post. It was a commodious dug-out and we took the opportunity of breaking up a bed—it was an evacuated German shelter, probably some headquarters or officers' quarters, and was well fitted—making a fire and brewing a little tea. We then moved on and came upon an English Battalion, standing in a well-made trench evacuated by the enemy and receiving its full share of attention from the German artillery. Here we learned that our Battalion was a little in front and we hurried to overtake them. We came to a slight mound, over which we were warned not to go, as a machine gun was firing right over it. However, we risked it, and got over quite all right, though we noticed several dead strewn about it. We found the Battalion settled in shell-holes behind the Canadians, and awaiting the word to "go over." As the platoon to which I belonged had not arrived, the company line had been spread out, and a re-arrangement became necessary. The positions we were intended to occupy were evacuated by the soldiers who

---

8   From the 29th August to the 3rd September, 1918, the 2nd Seaforths were attached to the Canadian Corps, First Army, and took part in the Battles of the Scarpe and Drocourt-Quent Line.

58

held them, and we moved up to take up our stance. Just as we did so, a machine gun opened fire right in our direction, and killed three corporals outright and wounded two private soldiers. Every man was hit in the neck, and all the corporals, strange to say, had only received their promotion before we set out on this venture. I do not know that it will be of much interest to my readers, but one of the wounded men was an Irishman who had just come from a military prison where he had served part of a two years' sentence for desertion, I believe. His wound proved a Blighty one, and after the armistice I noticed that he had been sentenced to a term of imprisonment in Dublin for committing bigamy. One of the corporals was a 1914 man, and had been wounded four times prior to his fatal wound, while another had been out since early in 1915, and had not been previously hit.

Tanks preceded the Canadians in this attack, but I do not know if they were very fortunate. When we went over we saw two or three coming back and passed several very badly damaged. One of those coming back was hit and went on fire. I believe some of the crew—I do not know how many were inside, but one or two were walking on behind—were literally roasted alive. "Whippet tanks," small, speedy, vicious machines, also accompanied the attack, and they were more successful. They were smartly handled and did some very fine and astonishing work. We followed the Canadians at a good pace, and in due course had to reinforce. They had been "hung up" by the wire in front of one trench and there had received many casualties, several of the bodies hanging over the wire riddled with bullets. Just past this wire I noticed two bodies, a Canadian and a German, in a horrible embrace. Each had bayonetted the other, and the points of the bayonets protruded out the backs of each. After they had fallen thus, they had evidently tried to grapple with each other (perhaps quite unintentionally) for their hands were stretched out and holding one another's clothes. We passed on and came to a village where we were brought up for a moment. At the remnants of a house near the end of the village a Hun stood watching! Down we lay and fired away, but without effect; so we crawled nearer, fired again, but he still stood, so we repeated this performance. Cautiously we approached till we were within rushing distance, when we charged up to find a German tunic filled with straw on which stood a steel helmet! That dummy had held us up about quarter of an hour!

The attack lasted until we had crossed over what we were told was the famous Hindenburg Line[9]. We passed this in the afternoon and proceeded on till we came to a wood, in front of which ran a sunken road, where we stopped. There was a village in front, but it was untenable, and as it was in a hollow, of no practical utility. The Germans, who had been for a number of years in this locality, had with great ingenuity utilised the shelter supplied by the wood for the erection of huts, while one side of the sunken road was lined with dug-outs, splendidly fitted. The huts looked as though they had been used for dining

---

[9]   Attached to XXII Corps, First Army, the 2nd Seaforths fought the Battle of the Canal du Nord between the 27th September and 1st October, 1918, and crossed the Hindenburg Line.

halls, though a few contained beds in which, no doubt, the bolder of the German occupants had spent their nights in preference to the foetid air of the dug-outs. There were in and around the huts dozens of wine bottles, but also alas! all were empty. Prior to settling here, we came across another sunken road in which there had been a French mortar battery of several guns, together with a large ammunition dump. A British shell had fallen there, and the dump had "gone up," with the result that there was a huge hole in the side of the road, while dead Germans strewed the road, many of them actually smouldering and smelling horribly of burnt flesh. A dug-out in this road was hissing furiously, and it had the general appearance of having been anything but a healthy locality at some period of that day! We had a large number of prisoners that day; I saw them marching down the line in large bodies, while our aid posts dealt with a huge mass of German wounded. The German killed strewed the terrain of the attack, and it showed how strong a rearguard action had been fought by the retiring enemy, for nearly all the dead were machine-gunners, who must have kept firing almost to the last man. One had to see to credit how ingeniously the guns were placed to give them the maximum of protection with the maximum of efficiency. Our casualties were heavy, certainly, but they were nothing compared to those of the Germans.

While there had been this little hell on earth, the air services of both countries had had a busy day. I saw several battles in the air, and some splendid work was done by the airmen on both sides. The German 'planes were well held, however, and several were driven down. I saw five aeroplanes come down in flames that day, two British and three German. The British machines were small, but the Germans were larger. One, indeed, carried a crew of four, and when the crew saw that there was no chance of bringing the aeroplane to earth, the men calmly walked out of the machine into space! It was a courageous cool act on the part of all the men, even though death was inevitable either way, whether they stayed where they were or "walked" out. One of the British machines made a valiant bid to get to earth and dashed down at a great pace, blazing furiously. When about 50 feet from the ground, however, and while the machine was being "flattened out" to land, something went wrong for the aeroplane crashed. I could not investigate any of these tragedies, of course, so do not know whether all who came down there were killed or not. Somehow, to me, an aeroplane in an attack always looked exceedingly cool, insolent and deadly earnest, probably because of the neat evolutions, the fact of the attacked machine rarely making a dash for freedom, even though, generally speaking, aeroplanes never fought one to one, and the fact that one usually fell.

I may mention that the Germans dammed a canal here and flooded the valley in which stood the village of which I made mention, so that the British occupied one ridge and the Germans the other, with a vast expanse of water between. The result was that both sides felt safe from attack, for no great mass of troops could have crossed over to drive off the Germans, nor could an attack develop until a tolerably safe passage was assured. The sector, therefore, was very quiet, for the artillery on both sides was not aggressively active, so that this countryside, so recently the scene of wild carnage became one of the most peaceable in the battle area at that time.

XXI
THE STORMING OF A VILLAGE IS A SOMEWHAT SERIOUS AFFAIR
24TH JULY, 1920

I AM SOMEWHAT mixed as to what happened after the events chronicled in the last article, but it is quite immaterial from the point of view of my readers, or so at least I imagine, for the focus of the happenings cannot be of much account to those who have not been "over there," the main interest centring on what took place. Needless to say we did not remain long in the sector over which we had newly advanced, but moved off to other scenes of violence and gave the Hun an extra push nearer home. The next place I have any clear recollection of was a small village beyond Cambrai, which had been taken by that time. The city was badly damaged, but we did not see much of it, as we were going forward to take up a position nearer the fighting area. I noticed one or two light field German pieces standing in little out-of-way-corners, which had had a tolerably wide range of fire, but which had not been drawn out quickly enough and had been captured by British infantry—showing, I think, that the British advance here had been much swifter than the enemy had anticipated. This was all the more wonderful when one remembers that, according to the official communiqué thereanent, the bridges approaching to Cambrai had been blown up and the troops had to cross over single planks! The streets of Cambrai were packed with troops of all sorts, motor lorries were running to and fro in miles, while all sorts of artillery, field and heavy, were being drawn up to the fighting areas. It was an inspiring sight and certainly brought home to one the insignificance of a single individual as a fighting unit.

We moved on and eventually reached our little village, which was in reach of artillery fire, but tolerably safe. Here we settled down for the night and a series of peculiar incidents happened which I think should be of interest. We had five accidents among the soldiers—more than I had ever seen for any one day among the troops, though, of course, it should be understood that, as is bound to be the case where there are large bodies of men, accidents were of fairly frequent occurrence. For instance, before we came here and while we were in hutments not far from the village where our Divisional Wing for the Arras front was wont to stand, we had two accidents—one man was badly kicked in the face by a horse and another ate a tinned pudding—bought from the canteen—and became a mild case of ptomaine poisoning.

In this particular village we had five accidents in the course of the night, all the men having to go to the hospital. The first to be brought in was a man who had been searching for what he could find in a wardrobe, when the wardrobe suddenly fell on top of him causing some damage to his chest. Two men started a wrestling match and the one who lost walked to the Aid Post with a broken collar bone. A transport wagon ran over the foot of one of the transport men, and he was a troublesome, very noisy patient, for a damaged foot is very painful. Another man was boiling a dixie of tea—the Army method of making tea was, usually, to put tea and water together, and bring the water to the boil—when something happened and the tea spilled on to his leg. Late in the night, or early next morning, the Aid Post had another casualty. A runner from Battalion Headquarters was sent with a message to a Company officer. He found the billet all right, and asked where the officer was sleeping. He was directed upstairs and went up. When he got to the top of the stairs he stepped forward and landed at the ground floor again. He had stepped into a shell hole where the floor should have been, and the result was a broken nose, damaged wrist, badly scratched leg and twisted back, not to mention two beautiful black eyes! The Aid Post staff did not spend a restful night.

The next morning we moved forward to our fighting position and commenced chasing the retreating Germans. I do not know if I mentioned it before, but there could be no doubt but that the retreat was orderly, and that the rearguard action the enemy fought was brilliant, though one could easily see costly. We were moving up in the direction of the Valenciennes sector and the district was well villaged. The storming of a village is a somewhat serious affair. There are always nooks and crannies in a village as well as peculiarly built houses which offer a fine field of fire. The ground had been in German hands for over four years and they had their machine guns placed to excellent advantage. The enemy, however, were considerate enough, generally speaking, to avoid bayonet work, and contented themselves with a hasty retreat or an ignominious surrender, but not before they had done all the damage possible with their machine guns. As soon as the enemy infantry were clear of the town or village the German artillery opened out on it, and spitefully, for the fire could serve no useful purpose, destroyed as much of it as they could before they had to pull out their artillery again. In these later days of the war, the Germans did not show any chastened spirit or promise of less Hunnish nature. They gave the people in a village the preference of going back with them or retiring towards the British lines; or, of course, of remaining where they were. A few went back with the Germans, and their journey was not an envious one, for our artillery was very strong, standing almost wheel to wheel, and was kept particularly busy day and night hammering away at the ground over which the retiring enemy had to pass. Those who retired on the British line also had a dangerous journey, for the German artillery and machine guns were working overtime to hamper our advance. We met countless refugees in these concluding phases of the war. There can be nothing more pathetic than to see these poor underfed people, excitement in every line of their figures, rushing along with barrows, hand carts and perambulators laden with such of their household goods as they could snatch together, trying to get out of the zone of fire, yet loth to leave their homes. Some, as I have indicated, were so loth that they did not leave their homes, and some, bedridden people could not. This the Germans well knew, yet, without reason, they loosed their artillery on these villages, with the full knowledge that the people on whose hospitality they had forced themselves for over four years would in all probability suffer from their shell fire. For utter callousness it would be hard to beat the following. In one village there were 47 people, mostly old, and many of them, through lack of proper treatment and food, confined to bed. The Germans had never supplied these civilians with gas masks, yet hardly had their troops been compelled to withdraw till the enemy bombarded the village with gas shells and incendiary shells. The people had been advised to keep to the cellars of the houses—nearly all houses in France have underground cellars—so that they were in just the best place to be trapped, for they could not know if the house above them took fire, while gas, being heavier than air, descended to the cellars. It happened, however, that our lads got into this village and one of the men attached to the Aid Post got the people out of the village and on the road to safety. To do this he had to run imminent risk himself, for he had to give his gas mask to each in turn and lead or wheel in a barrow each individual well clear of the village. One girl, who had stayed with her mother, showed utter carelessness of danger while they left the village. She strolled casually without the gas mask, singing cheerfully and paying not the slightest attention to the shell fire, which was tolerably fierce, or to the exhortations of her escort to "hurry up."

The first village we took was, I think, Sulzoir[10]. Hardly had we taken it and gone forward than we were driven out again, the Germans slipping out two tanks against one—rather an unexpected move. We were at the village again; however, and captured it finally, and I believe the two tanks were also captured intact. We did not advance much further that day, but dug in, and during this night there was a continuous heavy shell fire from both sides. We had a number of casualties, but nothing to the number inflicted on the R.F.A. behind us. Our Aid Post was kept very busy all through the night, there being rarely fewer than three casualties waiting attention all the time. We advanced early again in the morning, and the platoon to which I belonged was almost entirely wiped out within two minutes of our moving off. Three heavy shells fell right amongst us, and we had seven killed and the majority of the rest wounded. Some were very badly hit, one chap, already with three wound bars, having both his lungs pierced. He was a pathetic figure as he lay breathing through the holes in his chest, waiting the stretcher bearers for whom a busy night had brought no rest but additional labour. After this "push" we came back to Sulzoir, and there I made the acquaintance of an ancient hero. He was a grandfather and lived with his son, the father of a family of three daughters, the eldest of whom was 24.

---

10 Saulzoir is the more likely spelling. It is a small village near Valenciennes. On the armistice, the 2nd Seaforths, as part of the 4th Division, were in XXII Corps Reserve, to the south east of Valenciennes.

He was also a soldier of '70[11], and he was still a soldier. When in the early days of the war in 1914, he heard the boom of the enemy's guns coming towards the village he took a fowling piece he had, loaded up, and took up a stance outside the village. He had endeavoured to get some of the villagers to join him, but in vain, so he went alone. He kept his lonely vigil some three days and nights before the Boche arrived. Then he raised his fowling-piece and fired. He told me with gusto that he saw one Boche fall. He fired three shots when the Germans came upon him and seized him. He was imprisoned, but he was an old man, and he was soon liberated. When telling one this story, he shook his fist vigorously at his son who had not the manhood, he said, to back his father in his attempt to defend the village.

The son told me the same story and also added that his father was continually in trouble with the enemy as he refused to raise his cap to the German officers and N.C.O.s, and also because he refused to work in the fields, and was wont to steal all the food he could lay his hands upon. He was continually in and out of prison, but his eyes had not been dimmed and his figure was as erect as ever. He was a fine French specimen, and with his fowling-piece facing the German horde would have been splendidly emblematic of the spirit of France in this great struggle.

XXII
ARMISTICE
31ST JULY, 1920

I DO NOT remember the name of the village on which we advanced after we had captured Sulzoir, but I do remember that to approach thereto we had to cross a fairly broad stream, the bridge over which the Germans had blown up. We were following up an English Battalion, and they had come to the stream and stopped there. Our boys joined them there, but it was necessary to advance, and the English did not seem too keen to take to the water. We had a long, hefty youth, a second-Lieutenant in charge of a platoon, and he led his charges across, jumping into the water first. The current was fairly strong, and the water something over five feet deep at its greatest depth, while the bottom of the stream was, of course, very uneven. The only support across the water was a few strands of barbed wire overhead, to which the men had to cling as they crossed. All the men were soaked to the armpits at least, and several slipped and had a good ducking. This, it should be understood, was early in the day, and soaking as they were, the men had to take the village, in which there was very little resistance offered, and proceed further. All the time, also, there was continuous artillery, machine-gun and rifle fire, but our casualties were not particularly heavy as the enemy were in retreat. The men returned early the

---

[11]   The Franco–Prussian War of 1870.

following morning having spent the best part of 24 hours soaking wet. They were an uninspiring body of men as they lined up for their tot of rum at the close of their day's work.

With each Division there was a pioneer Battalion—a sort of works Battalion which, however, when occasion demanded had to go "over the top" with the rest of us or take their stand to assist a defence. I had always thought, in my ignorance, that the pioneer lot had a "soft" time all the time, but I quickly reversed my opinion in these later days of the war when, having become more used to things, I had or took every opportunity of seeing what was going on around me. Hardly had the first line of an attack advanced than the pioneer battalion was rushed up to repair the damaged roads and do kindred work, so that the transport necessary to do the successful carrying out of an attack might not be delayed. They came just when the enemy artillery, having failed to stem the attack, turned its attention to any reinforcements that might be coming up with a view to making them as weak as possible, so that the pioneer battalion, very often with little or no shelter, had to work away under conditions that were anything but favourable.

The field artillery men also had a particularly hard time towards the close of hostilities. The number of guns on the front was materially increased, so that the guns stood very close together. Naturally, the German artillery were always anxious to silence as many British pieces as possible, the result being that the artillery men suffered when the infantry were not undergoing anything like the danger with which they were faced. The promptitude with which the guns were moved up as the enemy retired was also astonishing to the infantryman who had believed that field guns always stood well back.

I noticed that there were fewer "slight" casualties at the close of the war—in the sector in which I was engaged, I mean—than at any time I had been at the front. There were fewer casualties, I should think, but the casualties were more serious, for the most part, being the result of shell fire rather than of machine-gun and rifle fire, for it naturally follows that an enemy in retreat, and not fighting a very stubborn rearguard action, cannot use rifles and only machine-guns up to a certain point. There can be no doubt but that the Germans knew that they were thoroughly beaten, for the Turks and Bulgars had by this time unconditionally surrendered[12], and the prisoners we took were quite confident that the German bid for power had finished. The people in the villages we took also informed us that the German officers, before retiring, had said that the German troops were outnumbered, some stating the figures at three to one, while the highest estimate I heard was ten to one. We, the infantry, did not believe all this, of course. We could not imagine that there was even a possibility of a cessation of hostilities. We could not, I think, imagine that the war would ever end except by ending each individual one—I mean that the end of the war had come to mean to the individual soldier the violent end of his

---

12 Bulgaria signed an armistice on 29th September, 1918, followed by Turkey on the 30th October, and Italy on the 3rd November.

own life, and the idea of conclusion by agreement of the Powers concerned seemed too good to be true.

I rather think that this was the last occasion on which we were actually employed as a fighting unit. We went back to Sulzoir and there rested for some little time and then proceeded to Valenciennes. While we were at Sulzoir the armistice was signed and the "cease fire" order given at 11 o'clock a.m. I happened to have gone on leave a day or two previously, so that I was in Blighty on Armistice Day, but I learned from the lads when I got back that the troops of our Battalion had only heard vague rumours and actually did not know that the armistice had been signed until they were awakened that night by the blare of two brass bands belonging to two other battalions of our Brigade. They went out to find out what was the matter, and only when, incredulous, they were told that peace had come did they notice the quiet of the night. No guns were firing, and only the music of the bands and the cheers of the soldiers broke the repose of the night. To celebrate the occasion two houses in the village were set on fire, and the soldiers roamed about making the night hideous with their joyous shouts. Peace had come, and that there might be no doubt about it, the boys were allowed a whole holiday the following day. The war had finished, and everybody was enthusiastic in the belief that soon they would be civilians again.

We moved from Sulzoir to Valenciennes, and there spent a fairly enjoyable time. Of course, there were parades, but these were of short duration, and life was tolerably smooth. It was in Valenciennes that we brought in the New Year. It is an Army custom that the English Regiments celebrate Christmas, while the Scottish Regiments hold their festivities at the New Year. On New Year's Eve there were no "lights out" and no roll call for our battalion, and all night in the Square our boys did the honours in true Highland spirit. The pipe band played out the bad old year and in the year of peace, while the soldiers danced and sang and imbibed the wine that the city could offer. Next day we had dinner, the feast to which we looked forward the whole year through, the importance of which was counted only second to leave, and after ample justice had been done to the bounteous fare, the various platoons formed up, and each headed by a piper, marched to a theatre where the Divisional Concert Party had been engaged to give a performance for our benefit. That march must have astonished the natives—indeed, the whole festivities must have convinced the people that there was still some joy in the world which had worn a cheerless face for them for over four years. Most of the men had dined well, and if asked, would no doubt have averred, wisely, that our march was really a triumphant one. After the visit to the theatre we returned for tea, and then dispersed. Some of our company raided a ration dump and helped themselves to a jar or two of rum, which they used to good effect, as I can testify, for I was in the Regimental Aid Post at the time, and we had no doctor—he having been demobilised—and I was taken to prescribe for more sore heads next morning than I remember having known of in any one company before. So ended—or rather began—the first year of peace, and the end of the year saw the dispersal of almost all the boys who formed our Battalion to their several homes.

XXIII
THE ARMY OF OCCUPATION
7TH AUGUST, 1920

WITH the armistice and the cessation of active hostilities these articles must necessarily close, for it was the endless vigil, the drab monotony and the sudden flashes of terrorising destruction which represented to the public of Britain the term "Doing One's Bit," and with the fact that men had ceased to be cannon fodder there came a "slump" in khaki and the soldiers for whom nothing was quite good enough in the days of war, were thrown on a country which could not even offer them the employment they required to live in even that mode of comfort to which they had been accustomed in pre-war days. And soldiers in the long hours of their agony had dreamed their dreams—dreams which they were encouraged to dream—of a land fit for heroes to live in, a land of homes, with all that homes meant for them who had lived among filth and discomfort for endless months, with plenty, and above all, with peace. Yet they returned to find no homes, no work, anything but plenty, and certainly no peace. Few cared very much, however, for the great personal menace had been beaten off and soldiers were just soldiers again, units of some Army of Occupation or other, and the demobilised soldiers were just ordinary people in "civvies." The days of the soldier's glory had died!

But this, as the writer of "Current Topics" would say is digression. The life of the soldier in the Army of Occupation was not at all a bad one. There was always the discipline and the hours of tedium, but on the whole time passed quickly enough, for units were continually moving about and an opportunity given to thousands to see that part of the Continent from Boulogne to the Rhine which most of them could have had but little hope of visiting but for the war. Then there always loomed in the distance the acme of the soldier's desire, his demobilisation. The methods of demobilisation were, as was to be expected, useless from every point of view. The matter could have been arranged perfectly and simply, but it was made complicated and anything but perfect. What should have been was to discharge all regular soldiers who had served over their colour service, and allowed a little time to lapse in order that they might be absorbed in the labour market; next all soldiers to whom work was open should have been liberated; thirdly, all other soldiers should have been set free according to service; and only then should unemployment "dole" have been issued, with restrictions as to whom it was to be paid. This would have saved the country hundreds of thousands of pounds, and would also have saved the soldiers much heart-burning. However, the Government decreed otherwise and the result was chaos.

The Battalion to which I was attached, removed from Valenciennes and proceeded to Binche, where we spent several months, and many of the soldiers formed friendships with the inhabitants of the town, which will last while life lasts. The people were very kind, and according to their means, were generous to the British soldiers, and especially friendly to us, who were the first kilted regiment they had ever seen. On our entry into the place the natives turned out en masse to welcome us, but principally, I think, to hear our pipe band, which was never without its appreciative audience whenever it made its appearance in the streets. The shop windows were decorated with placards bearing mottoes such as "Welcome to the heroes of Bapaume," "Your country is proud of you," and so forth, while bunting was displayed at the windows of houses of those people who had bunting to display. The Allied flags were all right, but a special mention might be given to the Union Jack which was fairly common—a fine confection in pink, white and pale blue. The people had been under German rule for over four years, and as a result they had practically nothing of real value left. The factories and workshops were idle, though the coalmines in this district continued to work as they had done during the time of the German occupation. The coal mines seemed to me, who knew but little of coal mines, to be worked on the most modern lines, and at each mine a large bath-house was erected where the miners changed from their working clothes to the more respectable habiliments of their home life. The clothes were attached to chains and were hoisted to the roof, each chain attached to it a disc bearing the owner's name, and a padlock of which the owner had the key. Some twenty or thirty shower baths were provided, each divided from the other by a partition, so that the men had a measure of privacy. These miners were the only workpeople who could have any but the barest existence, the residue of the population, except the wealthier inhabitants, having to subsist, for the most part, on the rations issued to them from convenient centres. At every meal time the soldiers were mobbed by women and children with all sorts of receptacles in which to carry away the "buckshee."

In time we moved from Binche, some going "on demob," and others to Germany. Finally, my turn came and I was sent to Duren, a fair sized German city, well filled with soldiers. At Duren the life was different. The people were different, naturally, and we were forbidden to "fraternise." The shops were well supplied with goods, but the prices were pretty high. So far as I could see, and I had to judge here from outside appearances, the people were not nearly so badly off as the people on whom they had lived for four years in France and Belgium, but their "tone" was not quite so good, probably owing to the fact that they were and felt themselves a conquered people. I was in several villages in turn after this, most of which seemed to be fairly prosperous, but all had suffered from the war, as could be seen from the number of photographs one saw of sailors and soldiers draped with crepe. The women folk had not been behind any more than had been the women of Britain, and I saw several photographs of munition workers, nurses, hospital attendants, etc., but not many "land girls," as it seemed to be the custom in Germany as in Shetland for women to do the heaviest land work without earning, either before, during, or after the war, a word of praise from anyone. Perhaps they lack the praise because they do not wear breeches!

While in Germany I took the opportunity offered by the Army Authorities by way of river excursions, to visit several cities on the Rhine, and I had previously taken the chance of a ten days' leave in Paris, and a week's leave in Brussels, so that I certainly made the most of my trip to the Continent. From what I saw of them the Germans are a hard-headed business-like, thorough people, and there is no doubt but that the nation, despite the demands made upon them by the Allies, and the continued efforts of France to ruin the country, will continue to be a great power in the world. Of course everyone knows of the charges made against the Germans in respect of the war. I have no admiration for war of any kind, but I do object to charges of cruelty being made against an enemy. War is war, and the rules laid down at any Convention for fighting a war are merely ridiculous and made to be broken. When a nation enters on war, that nation enters on a very serious business and not a piece of sport, and the business is to get the thing finished as soon as possible. Any means which can accomplish this end will always be used by one side or the other, and, if war is going to continue, as to all appearance it is, it would be well for the peoples of all nations to understand this fact, so that they might be prepared in the event of war, for every form of cruelty and savage destruction that the ingenuity of man can devise. A victorious Army, as was Germany's in the first days of the war, is a savage Army, and every man no doubt felt regal in his power, and a beaten Army, as Germany's at last became, is like a cornered animal, and will do anything to regain the upper hand. There is but one way to face war successfully, and it is for each individual to hold life as no value, to have callous contempt for death, and to fear neither the suffering one must undergo nor the suffering of others. It is a big inhuman demand to make on anyone, but war is really the most inhuman relic still left of medieval times. A League of Nations to make peace is useless unless it can make war, and war in the fiercest, most terrifying form, for no people anxious to expand in power or territory, will ever be content to abide by the decision of a body which cannot back up that decision by all the majesty of might.

For the most part the Germans were disposed to be tolerably friendly, but occasionally there was a little trouble. I saw in one or two places notices in the windows of the municipal offices to the effect that certain Germans had been sentenced for varying terms for endeavouring to spread disaffection among the soldiers, but these cases were not common. In one town I took part in a "row" with some Germans, who had tackled a young band boy. I presume he had given the natives some "cheek," and when they started to chastise him his shouts brought others on the scene and a little riot ensued. In another village a British soldier was stabbed in a wood. I do not know the wherefore, but I imagine there was provocation. I can only suggest that this might be a case where the words of the famous Frenchman would apply—"Cherchez la femme." At any rate the other soldiers stationed thereabout were very wroth about this affair, and one night went into the town—after they should have been in their billets—and laid about them lustily to such effect that, I think, seven Germans were killed and several severely injured. Several of our lads served terms of imprisonment for this "escapade," their attempts at revenge proving rather disastrous for themselves. In due course I was demobilised and came to Britain and shortly afterwards home. With that ended my life as a soldier and with that too must end my articles.

XXIV
PEACE IS INTERNATIONAL
14TH AUGUST, 1920

I HAVE TRIED to give to my readers some idea of the kind of life a soldier led when there was a war on. My descriptions have not reached my ideal, and I have been unable to make a living picture of the horrors the boys endured, but I have written sufficient, I think, to show that the life of the trenches, in that shell-shattered strip of France from the coast to Switzerland was not one to leave a man glowing with pride in his heroism, or filled with the spirit of self-sacrifice, determined to die, or worse still, to be mutilated and live, in order that that nebulous thing, civilisation, which he thought he understood but found he didn't, might be preserved. The whole experience taught him one thing and one thing only, and that was the innate wrongness of war, with a huge wastage of the manhood and wealth of the countries involved, and its train of abysmal brutishness, its unnatural callousness, and its aftermath of hate. Those men who fought never want to fight again. They never want to suffer the discomforts of mud and vermin again. They want peace, they want comfort, which means that they want work and reasonably paid work; and they want time for recreation. All these things they want, but they have not got them yet, and like the baby and the Pear's soap, they won't be happy till they get them. A great deal was written and said about the democratic Army of the fighting period. It was not a democratic Army. It was run just very much on the same lines as the old Army, the Army of the South African War and the peace-time Army after that. The fact that a ranker could apply for and receive a Commission did not make the Army any more democratic than when commissioned rank was only open to the nobility and well-to-do. I have nothing to say against the Army. The British Army is the best Army there is, and the British Tommy is looked after and "mothered" better than any other soldier, but still that does not make it a democratic Army, any more than the American Army or the Canadian, Australian, New Zealand or South African contingents of the British Army. The nearest approach to a democratic Army I know is the Sinn Fein Army—if army it can be called—and it is democratic in so far as it is composed of men everyone of whom has but a single thought, with the rightness or wrongness of which it is not my province to deal with here, which thought each individual is determined to see a realised fact at whatever cost.

This matter, of a democratic Army is, however, an aside. Yet it may not be an aside; it may be that it is the solution. For the first great necessity to the tortured world is peace, and it is a world peace that the man who knows war wants to see. Peace is a national matter, but more than that it is international. A League of Nations is a beautiful idea, and one that should at least have a fair trial; but its weakness lies in the fact that there can be no guarantee that the nations composing the League may not themselves quarrel. A democratic Army, where every man is a soldier, may be a good idea, but its weakness is that such an Army is apt to breed militarism, while it naturally follows that the country or Empire with the greatest number of men and the greatest wealth, becomes a menace to the rest of the world. The only real solution is the total disarmament of the world, the disbanding of every fighting unit, and the conversion of factories for the manufacture of weapons of war into workshops for the manufacture of the tools of peace. The glamour of war must be killed and the children of the world taught that there is no glamour, only torture and grief, only death and desolation. But these things must be international and world wide, though there is no reason why our school books with their savage glorying in the bloodshed of the past should not now be scrapped and rewritten in such a spirit that the children learning from them might grow up determined that there shall be no more war. That would be a step in the right direction, and with the coming of a world peace there should also come a world prosperity.

It is, indeed, a hard thing that the men who did fight should now have to go idle. There could be work in plenty for them, enough work on the land alone to absorb a large percentage of them, for they know, as everyone knows who reads the newspapers, that huge tracts of land cultivated during the war to supply the needs of the country, are now uncultivated in order that prices may be maintained, and that at a time when unemployment is rampant in the land, and when people are finding difficulty in making ends meet because of high prices. There is little wonder that discontent is rife in the land when such things can happen. It was not to enable a section of the community to exploit the rest that these men fought, but the reason of their fighting and the actual results that have been obtained are not even on nodding acquaintance. We are said to be on the verge of war with Russia. With every other thinking person, I hope there will be no war. But should it come, can the Government of the country, and the Government is the people, hope that these men, treated as they have been treated, and knowing what they know of war and the results thereof, they will freely come forward and offer to give up everything with the knowledge that, if they do not, their reward will be the same as was their reward at the conclusion of the Great War? It is inconceivable to me that such would be the case. The manhood of the country remember too vividly the horrors and discomforts, the "death that flieth by night," the vermin and the eternal soul-destroying digging of refractory earth, to be again gulled by the glamour so skilfully thrown round the destruction called war. Their patriotism is a constructive and not a destructive patriotism, and, though, of course many might go "to defend their country," their stake in which is so small that it cannot guarantee them work on their return from fighting, the majority will reply, to any policy of foreign strife, "Na poo!"

I know that in the course of writing these articles I have made mistakes. I have missed out parts that might well have been written, and have not transferred to paper the vividness of the actual happenings as I should like to have done. If I have been lurid at times, I have not been lurid enough; if I have ever painted a scene that looked peaceful or savouring of rest and contentment, I have erred. There were times of quiet, but never times of peace; there were days of rest, but never days of contentment. I once saw a common yellow butterfly on a bright spring morning, settle on the side of a trench and flutter along it for a bit, and it drew quite a little crowd of admirers round it. I once heard a bird whistle once or twice near a trench and saw it sitting on a blasted tree, and all the men within hearing remarked on it. A flower blooming in the side of a trench was a wonder of perennial interest to all who saw it. Common things, Nature's most common handiwork, became marvels, miracles, when seen "in the line." That was what life in the trenches was like. No criminal in these days suffers for his crime what the soldiers suffered in their fight against the Germans. Life itself became a punishment; a wound was almost prayed for in order that life might become endurable. I wonder if my readers can imagine such a state? In order that a man might have some measurement of contentment and laughter in his life he desired that his flesh might be lacerated? Can any reward great enough be offered men who endured such a life? Yet they do not ask for a reward. They only ask for work and fair dealing. And they don't get that. As the Americans say, Can you beat it?

This article may read like the wail of a malcontent, but it is for the fighting men I plead. I know nothing of the Navy. I knew nothing of what the men who manned our ships endured, so that I cannot speak for them. But of the soldiers who fought through smiling, and it is for them I plead. It is a fine thing to raise a monument in memory of the dead, it is a fine thing to know that the maimed have sufficient on which to live, it is a fine thing to know that the soldier's widow and the soldier's orphans receive their mode of care, but it would be a splendid thing to know that the living, unpensioned soldier had the ordinary fair treatment to which he is entitled by all the canons of British fairplay, and to know that he had, not only work to do, but reasonable hours and a sufficient wage on which to procure the warmth and comfort of which he dreamed in the muddy trenches on a winter night in France and Flanders.

APPENDIX 1

Shetland Seaforth Highlanders in The Great War

From *Shetland's Roll of Honour and Roll of Service* T & J Manson, Lerwick, 1920

SHETLAND SEAFORTHS ROLL OF HONOUR

Where possible additional details have been added to the original text of *Shetland's Roll of Honour and Roll of Service*.
Any inaccuracies and omissions are entirely the fault of the editor.

Thomas Aitken, Private, S/14530, 8th Seaforth Highlanders. Son of the late Wm. and Catherine Aitken, Hoolls, Burra Isle. Killed in action near Arras, France, Sunday 23rd April, 1917. Aged 40. He is buried at Guemappe British Cemetery, Wancourt, France.

James L. Blance, Lance-Corporal, S/12543, 8th Battalion Seaforth Highlanders. Only son of James and Clementina Blance, Norna's Court, Lerwick. Killed in action in France on Sunday 22nd July, 1918. Aged 25 years. He is buried in Royallieu French National Cemetery, Compiegne.

Andrew Byrne, Private, S/6241, 7th Seaforths. Son of Mrs Jane Byrne, 1 Stove's Buildings, Lerwick. Killed in action in France on Monday 18th July, 1916. Aged 24 years. His name is on the Thiepval Memorial, France, Pier and Face 15c.

John Smith Cutt, Corporal, 241050, 5th Seaforth Highlanders. Son of Mr William and Mary Cutt, St Mary's Holm, Kirkwall, Orkney, formerly Lower Lochside, Lerwick. Killed in action in France, on Monday 9th April, 1918. Aged 22 years. His name is recorded on the Arras Memorial, France, Bay 8.

Thomas Cutt, Private, 5296, 5th Seaforth Highlanders. Son of Mr William and Mary Cutt, St Mary's Holm, Kirkwall, Orkney, formerly Lower Lochside, Lerwick. Died of gas poisoning in France, Thursday 27th July, 1916. Aged 22 years. He is buried in Dernancourt Communal Cemetery, France.

Louis Drummond Don, S/41860 Private "A" Coy.1-6th Batt. Seaforth Highlanders. Youngest son of Rev. Mathew and Annie Don, The Manse, Whalsay. Killed in action, Tuesday 27th August, 1918, in the Battle of the Scarpe, near Roeux, 5 miles east of Arras. Aged 19. He is buried in Brown's Copse Cemetery, Roeux, France.

John Henry, Private, S/25065, 4th Seaforth Highlanders. Only son of William Henry, Gossamedow, Foula. Died of pneumonia in Edinburgh, on 23rd July, 1918. Aged 18. He is buried in Edinburgh (Comely Bank) Cemetery. In the Commonwealth War Graves Register, Private Henry is listed as being a Gordon Highlander and this is most likely to be accurate.

William Andrew Henry, Private, S/16157, 2nd Seaforth Highlanders. Son of Mrs Joan and the late James Henry, Bridge of Walls. Killed in action at Arras, on Wednesday 11th April, 1917. Aged 24. He is buried in Brown's Copse Cemetery, Roeux, France.

Alex G. Sandison Ingram, 14918, Lance Corporal, 8th Seaforth Highlanders. Only son of Mr and Mrs Walter Ingram, 7, Albany Street, Lerwick, formerly 47 St Olaf Street. Killed in action at Ypres, Belgium, on Tuesday 31st July, 1917. Aged 21. His name is recorded on the Menin Gate Memorial, Ypres, Belgium, Panel 38.

Peter J. Inkster, Private, S/18971, 2nd Seaforth Highlanders Labour Corps. Son of A. Inkster, Houll, North Roe. Died of Uraemic Coma on Wednesday 3rd April, 1918, at No. 2 General Hospital, Havre, France. Aged 38 years. He is buried at Ste. Marie Cemetery, Le Havre, France.

John Scott Irvine, Lance-Corporal, S/11452, 10th Seaforth Highlanders. Only son of Mr and Mrs Andrew Irvine, New Road Scalloway. Died of meningitis at the Fever Hospital, Dunfermline, Thursday 17th August, 1916. Aged 18 years. He is buried in Dunfermline Cemetery.

Bertie Jamieson, Private, S/24844, Seaforth Highlanders. Son of Mr and Mrs John Jamieson, 3, Reform Lane, Lerwick, formerly Uyeasound, Unst. Died at home, of pleurisy, Thursday 18th July, 1918. Aged 19. He is buried in Lerwick New Cemetery.

Robert Jamieson, Private, 202266, 4th Seaforth Highlanders. Elder son of the late Robert and Elizabeth Jamieson, Swinister, Ollaberry. Died of pneumonia on Monday 28th May, 1917, at Norfolk War Hospital, Norwich. Aged 27. He is buried in Ollaberry Kirkyard.

R G Jamieson, Private, S/21057, 1/4th Seaforth Highlanders. Son of James and Barbara A. Jamieson, Lerwick. Died Friday 12th April, 1918, aged 28. He is buried in Étaples Military Cemetery, France.

James Johnson, Private, S/12967 "A" Coy. 6th Seaforth Highlanders. Son of Mr Thomas and Mrs Jessie Johnson, 3 Church Lane, Lerwick. Reported missing 31st August, 1918. His name is recorded on the Vis-En-Artois Memorial, Pas de Calais, France.

Thomas Hawick Johnson, Lance-Corporal, 202717, 4th Seaforth Highlanders. Husband of Mary Elizabeth Johnson, 46 Braewick Road, Lerwick, formerly Hillhead, Ollaberry, Northmavine. Son of the late James and Barbara Jameson Johnson. Killed in action on 20th July, 1918, near Marfaux, South-West of Rheims. Aged 35 years. He is buried in Marfaux British Cemetery, Marne, France.

William Johnston, Private, S/16490, 6th Battalion Seaforth Highlanders. Son of Mr and Mrs William Johnston, 4, Stove's Buildings, Lerwick. Killed in action on Tuesday 9th April, 1918, in France. Aged 20 years. His name is recorded on the Loos Memorial, France, Panel 112 to 115.

David Robertson Lawrence, Private, S/12545 8th Seaforth Highlanders. Son of Mr Wm. and Mrs Rossanna Lawrence, Hayes, by Virkie, formerly Home Farm, Sumburgh. Killed in action in France, Saturday 14th October, 1916. Aged 32 years. His name is inscribed on the Thiepval Memorial, France, Pier and Face 15c.

Frederick "Fred" L.F. Leisk, Private, S/25541, 6th Seaforths. Son of Jane and the late Peter Leisk, Glenfarquhar, formerly 12 Ronald Street, Lerwick. Reported missing, March, 1918, died Saturday 23rd March, 1918, aged 30. His name is inscribed on the Arras Memorial, France, Bay 8.

Robert Leask, Private, S/12948, 8th Seaforth Highlanders. Nephew of Robert Leask, Upper Lochside, Lerwick. Grandson of Margaret Leask, North Road, Lerwick. Died of wounds in France on Wednesday 21st September, 1916. Aged 25 years. He is buried in Etaples Military Cemetery, Pas de Calais, France.

Thomas Leask, Private, S/12643, 8th Seaforth Highlanders. Son of Robert and Elizabeth Leask; husband of Elizabeth Cooper Leask, Upper Lochside, Lerwick. Killed in action in the Somme Battle on Wednesday 11th October, 1916. Aged 19 years. His name is recorded on the Thiepval Memorial, France, Pier and Face 15c.

Karl Manson, Private, 242010, 5th Seaforth Highlanders. Second son of Thomas and Margaret E. Manson, *Shetland News*, Hillhead, Lerwick. Killed in action at the Battle of Arras, Monday 9th April, 1917. Aged 17 years. He is buried in Highland Cemetery, Roclincourt, France, with the inscription "What matters time if he fulfilled God's purpose in the day of need."

John Morrison, Private, S/12691, 8th Seaforth Highlanders. Son of Robert and Clementina Morrison, South Wart, Reawick. Killed in action in France on Monday 17th September, 1916. Aged 24 years. His name is recorded on the Thiepval Memorial, France, Pier and Face 15c.

Robert Morrison, Lance-Corporal, S/12692, 8th Seaforth Highlanders. Son of Robert and Clementina Morrison, South Wart, Reawick. Reported missing on Wednesday 22nd Aug., 1917. Aged 20 years. His name is recorded on the Tyne Cot Memorial, Zonnebeke, West-Vlaanderen, Belgium.

James J. Nelson, Private, S/8103, 1st Batt. Seaforth Highlanders, son of James C. Nelson, Old Dowie Farm, by Carnoustie (formerly of Hillswick). Killed in action in the Persian Gulf, on Friday 7th January. His name is recorded on the Basra Memorial, Iraq. Panel 37 64.

Thomas Newlands, Private, S/17859, 1st/6th Seaforth Highlanders. Son of Mr and Mrs Isaac Newlands, Greenfield, Orkney, formerly of Lerwick. Killed in action in Champagne, Sunday 21st July, 1918. Aged 19 years. He is buried in La Neuville-aux-Larris Military Cemetery, Marne, France.

John Blair Nisbet, Jr., Private, S/25800, 3rd Seaforth Highlanders, eldest son of John and Grace Nisbet, Scraefield, Balliasta, Baltasound, Unst. Died of Enteric Fever at Unst on Tuesday 21st January, 1919. Aged 21 years. He is buried in Balliasta Old Churchyard. Although recorded as a Seaforth in the Roll of Honour, Private Nisbet is listed as being in "H" Coy, 3rd Battn. Gordon Highlanders in the Commonwealth War Graves register. In the photograph in the Roll of Honour he does seem to be wearing a Gordons' cap badge.

Gideon Anderson Peterson, Private, 204237, 1/5th Seaforth Highlanders. Son of Robina A. and the late Peter Peterson, Setter, North Roe. Killed by the bursting of a shell at the Marne, on Tuesday 23rd July, 1918. Aged 24 years. He is buried in Marfaux British Cemetery, France.

John James Peterson, Private, S/12614, 8th Seaforth Highlanders, Second son of James and Barbara Peterson, 29 Rosemount Place, Aberdeen, formerly of Nesbister, Whiteness. Killed by the explosion of a shell while in the trenches, France, Sunday 15th October, 1916. Aged 19 years. His name is recorded on the Thiepval Memorial, France, Pier and Face 15c.

Peter Peterson, Private, 3/8104, 7th Seaforth Highlanders, son of Laurence and Elizabeth Peterson, Hillswick. Killed in action in France, on Wednesday 12th July, 1916. Aged 26 years. His name is recorded on the Thiepval Memorial, France, Pier and Face 15c.

Francis Pottinger, Private, 3/16343, 3rd Seaforth Highlanders. Son of Mr William and Mrs Annie Pottinger, Brettabister, N. Nesting. Died of meningitis at the Military Hospital, Cromarty, on Wednesday 2nd May, 1917. Aged 19 years. He is buried in Garth Old Churchyard.

William Pottinger, Private, S/13339, 1st Batt. Seaforth Highlanders. Son of Mr William and Mrs A.J. Pottinger, Setter, Burra Isle. Died of Dysentry at Amara, Mesopotamia, on Tuesday 9th January, 1917. Aged 22 years. He is buried in Amara War Cemetery, Iraq, on the left bank of the Tigris.

John Manson Sandison, Private, S/16996, 7th Seaforth Highlanders. Son of Andrew and Mary Sandison, Sandwick, Hillswick. Killed by a shell at Gouzeaucourt, on Tuesday 7th August, 1917. Aged 21 years. He is buried at Ruyaulcourt Military Cemetery, France.

Robert Sinclair, Lance-Corporal, S/16029, 2nd Seaforth Highlanders. Son of John Strong and Martha Sinclair, Hoswick, Sandwick. Died from wounds in Military Hospital, Woking, on Thursday 24th May, 1917. Aged 24 years. He is buried in Sandwick Parish Churchyard.

William Sinclair, Lance-Corporal, S/10491, 1st Seaforth Highlanders. Son of the late John and Mrs Sinclair, Rerwick, Dunrossness. Killed in action in Mesopotamia, Thursday 22nd February, 1917. Aged 21 years. His name is inscribed on the Basra Memorial, Iraq, Panel 37 and 64.

William Stephen, Private, 10502, 1st Seaforth Highlanders. Son of Mrs Jessie Stephen, Lyndhurst, Fort Road, Lerwick. (formerly of Brough, Bressay). Killed in action in France, Sunday 9th May, 1915. Aged 26 years. His name is recorded on the Le Touret Memorial, France.

Angus Wishart, Private, S/17704, 8th Seaforth Highlanders. Son of James Wishart, Stow, Eshaness, Northmavine. Killed at Ypres on Tuesday 28th August, 1917. Aged 23 years. He is buried in Aeroplane Cemetery, Belgium.

Andrew Williamson, S/7482, Private, 2nd Seaforth Highlanders. Son of Mrs Lilias Williamson, 20 Church Lane, Lerwick. Reported missing Saturday 1st July, 1916. Aged 21. His name is recorded on the Thiepval Memorial, France, Pier and Face 15c.

John Charles Williamson, Private, S/7481, 2nd Seaforth Highlanders. Son of the late Mr and Mrs Williamson, Ladysmith, Scalloway. Died of wounds in France, Wednesday 8th September, 1915. Aged 18 years. He is buried in Beauval Communal Cemetery, France.

Robert G. Williamson, Private, S/29919, Seaforth Highlanders. Charlotte Lane, Lerwick, son of Mrs Margaret Williamson of 46 Albany Street, Leith, Edinburgh. Died at home, January 1920. The Commonwealth War Graves Register states that Private Williamson died on Sunday 7th December, 1919. He is buried in Lerwick New Cemetery.

SHETLAND SEAFORTHS ROLL OF SERVICE

PARISH OF UNST

John Burns, Private, Seaforth Highlanders, Baltasound.

Frederick Jamieson, Lce.-Corporal, Seaforth Highlanders. Formerly of Uyeasound.

Thomas Jamieson, Sergeant, 1st Seaforths (Regulars). Formerly of Uyeasound. Wounded three times: at Ypres, October, 1917; on the Somme, September, 1916; and at Passchendaele Ridge, November, 1917. Decorations - Military Medal, Mons Star, and Delhi Durbar.

Alexander Priest, Private, Seaforth Highlanders. Stove, Haroldswick. Twice wounded in France, 24th July, 1918, 27th November, 1918. Decoration - Military Medal.

Laurence W. Smith, Private, 2nd Seaforth Highlanders. Haroldswick, Unst. Wounded at Ypres, Belgium, on 4th October, 1917.

PARISH OF YELL

James Clark, Private, Seaforth Highlanders. Littlester, Burravoe.

William Humphray, Private, Seaforth Highlanders. Brough, Burravoe. Wounded on 16th May, 1917 on the Arras Front.

James J. Nicolson, Lance-Corporal, Seaforth Highlanders. Kirkabister, Mid Yell.

William J. Williamson, Private, Seaforth Highlanders. Burravoe.

PARISH OF NORTHMAVINE

Peter Garrick, Private, 6th Seaforths. Ollaberry.

Robert Johnson, Seaforth Highlanders. Wounded on the Somme, 25th September, 1917. Stucca, Hillswick.

Arthur Peterson, Private, Seaforth Highlanders. Hillswick.

Andrew M. Sandison, Private, 4th Seaforth Highlanders (51st Division). East Hogaland, Ollaberry. Wounded on 12th October, 1916, and 22nd July, 1918.

Arthur Laurence Smith, Private, 1-5th Seaforth Highlanders. Islesburgh. Wounded at Arras on 6th September, 1918.

Alexander Tulloch, Private, 6th Seaforth Highlanders. Crugans, Northmavine. Wounded at Cambrai on 25th October, 1918.

PARISH OF DELTING

Alexander Murray, Private, Seaforth Highlanders. Hoya, Mossbank.

PARISH OF NESTING, LUNNASTING, WHALSAY AND SKERRIES

Nesting and Lunnasting

Laurence Pottinger, Private, Seaforth Highlanders. Railsburgh, South Nesting.

Robert Thomson, Private, Seaforth Highlanders. Orgill, Vidlin. Wounded in France, February, 1918.

Whalsay and Skerries

Alexander Sinclair, Private, 1st Seaforth Highlanders. Symbister.

Hercules Williamson, Private, 1st Seaforth Highlanders. Symbister.

PARISH OF SANDSTING AND AITHSTING

Sandsting

John Peterson, Private Seaforth Highlanders. Gruting Schoolhouse, Bridge-of-Walls. Wounded in France on 3rd May, 1917, and 18th October, 1918.

Peter Tulloch, Private, 8th Seaforth Highlanders. Skeld.

Aithsting

Mitchell Georgeson, Private, Seaforth Highlanders. East Houlland, Bixter.

Magnus Johnston, Private, Seaforth Highlanders. West Burrafirth, Aithsting. Wounded twice in Belgium, October, 1917, and April, 1918.

Magnus Laurenson, jun., Private, Seaforth Highlanders. West Burrafirth, Aithsting.

Peter J. Leslie, Private, 1-5th Seaforth Highlanders. Sandsound. Wounded in France on 23rd March, 1918, and 13th October, 1918.

Archibald Nicolson, Private, Seaforth Highlanders. Twatt, Aithsting.

PARISH OF WALLS, SANDNESS, PAPA STOUR AND FOULA

Walls

William Andrew Johnston, Private, Seaforth Highlanders. Kurkigarth.

John MacCullie, Lance-Corporal, 9th and 6th Seaforth Highlanders. Happyhansel Schoolhouse. Wounded at Albert on 27th March, 1918, and gassed south of Cambrai, on 26th October, 1918.

PARISH OF TINGWALL, WHITENESS AND WEISDALE

Tingwall

Joseph Hunter, Private, Seaforth Highlanders. Girlsta House, Girlsta. Wounded at Ypres, 1918. Once gassed.

Alex D. Leask, Private, 3rd Seaforths. Wadbister, Girlsta. Twice wounded at Arras and Cambrai.

Scalloway

Jas. Burgess, Private, Seaforth Highlanders. Midshore.

Walter James Cromarty, Lance-Corporal, Seaforth Highlanders. "Seaview." Wounded on 27th July, 1918, at Soissons.

William Scott, Private, Seaforth Highlanders. New Street.

PARISH OF LERWICK

Burgh and Landward Division

John Anderson, Corporal, 1-6th Seaforth Highlanders. 30 Albany Street. Wounded at Albert on 15th September, 1915.

William G. Anderson, Private, Seaforth Highlanders. 86 Commercial Street.

James L. Bolt, Private, 2nd Seaforth Highlanders. Ellensgowan, Gulberwick. Wounded at Arras on 28th March, 1918.

John Bolt, Private, Seaforth Highlanders. 5 Park Lane.

Sammy Cutt, Private, Seaforth Highlanders. Lower Lochside.

John M. Davidson, Lance-Corporal, 1-5th Seaforth Highlanders. 112 Commercial Street.

James Douglas, Corporal, 8th Seaforth Highlanders. 6 Market Street. Wounded at Buzancy on 28th July, 1918.

Samuel Gray, Signaller, 2nd Seaforths. 84a Commercial Street. Wounded at La Bassée, 10th April, 1918.

William Greig, Lance-Corporal, B.Coy., 3rd Seaforth Highlanders. 7 Albany Street. Wounded in France on 24th December, 1917.

R.M. Greig, Corporal, 5th Cameron Highlanders and 2nd Seaforth Highlanders, ex R.A.M.C. Queen's Lane.

Donald Gunn, Sergeant, 2nd Seaforths. Union Street. Gassed in France, 1917.

Charles C. Hay, Captain, 7th Battalion, Seaforth Highlanders. King Harald Street. Decoration - 1914-15 Star.

Thomas Jamieson, Private, Seaforths. 3 Reform Lane. Wounded in hand and leg.

William Jamieson, Private, Seaforth Highlanders. 3 Reform Lane.

John B. Johnston, Corporal, Seaforth Highlanders. Seafield Court.

Laurence L. Johnson, 7th Seaforths. South Shurton, Gulberwick.

William E. Johnston, Private, Seaforth Highlanders. 1 Burgh Road. Wounded in France, 14th October, 1916.

Magnus Mackay, Private, 1st Seaforth Highlanders. 18 Commercial Street.

Thomas A. Morrison, Private, Seaforth Highlanders. 41 Burgh Road. Injured by torpedoing of s.s. "St. Magnus."

John B.H. Murray, Private, Seaforth Highlanders. 31, Burns Lane. Wounded, April, 1917, at Arras.

Magnus P. Murray, Private, Seaforths. 31, Burns Lane.

William Murray, Private, Seaforths. 1, Burgh Road.

Henry L. Nicolson, Lance-Corporal, 4th Seaforths. Garths, Gulberwick.

John L. Robertson, Private, 9th Seaforths. 4 Freefield. Gassed at Kemmel Hill in April, 1918.

Andrew W. Smith, Private, 1st Batt., Seaforth Highlanders. Islesburgh House.

Francis C. Smith, Private, Seaforth Highlanders. 9 Market Street. Wounded on 31st July, 1917, at Ypres.

John R.A. Steven, Lance-Corporal, 6th Seaforth Highlanders. Freefield. Wounded and taken prisoner on 25th March, 1918. Decorations - M.M.

James Stout, Private, 2nd Battalion, Seaforth Highlanders. Medical Hall. Wounded in the Battle of Arras on 11th April, 1917.

John Tait, Private, Seaforth Highlanders. St. Magnus Street.

Thomas Tulloch, Sergeant, Seaforth Highlanders. Glengarth Villa. Wounded in France, April, 1917.

Burra

Thomas G. Pottinger, Private, Seaforth Highlanders. Branchiclate, Burra Isle. Wounded on 3rd May, 1917, at Rouai, France.

PARISH OF DUNROSSNESS

Sandwick and Levenwick

James Nicolson, Private, 2nd Seaforth Highlanders. Sandwick. Wounded at Arras on 24th April, 1917; at La Bassée on 14th July, 1918; and at Cambrai on 1st September, 1918.

Laurence G. Stove, Private, Seaforth Highlanders. Central, Sandwick Parish. Wounded at Kemmel Hill on 22nd April, 1918, and at Castrie on 6th June, 1918.

Donald J. Sutherland, Private, 1-6th Seaforth Highlanders. Swinister, Shetland. Wounded at Arras, 14th April, 1917, and October 1917.

Dunrossness

James A. Cumming, Private, 3rd Seaforth Highlanders. Sumburgh.

William Moncrieff, Signaller, Seaforth Highlanders. Spiggie, Dunrossness.

APPENDIX 2

Useful Contacts

The Commonwealth War Graves Commission,
2 Marlow Road,
Maidenhead,
Berkshire.
SL6 7DX

Tel: 01628 634221
Fax: 01628 771208
E-mail: cwgc@dial.pipex.com

Web Site: www.cwgc.org

The Commonwealth War Graves Commission maintains the graves and memorials to the 1.7 million members of the now Commonwealth forces who died during the two world wars. The Commission offers an enquiry service to the public whereby the exact place of a burial or commemoration for any casualty can be found. More complex searches on hometown or regiment are also available. In addition, the Commission's records are available on a search by surname basis only via the Commission's web site. For a full list of publications and services on offer, write to the above address.

The Western Front Association,
P.O. Box 1914,
Reading,
Berks.
RG4 7RG

Web site: www.westernfront.co.uk

The Western Front Association was formed to maintain interest in the Great War. Its main aim is to perpetuate the memory, courage and comradeship of all those, on both sides, who served their countries in France and Flanders. It does not seek to glorify war, is non-political, and welcomes members of all ages. Their excellent 'Stand To!' journal is posted to all members thrice a year. Their Historical Information Officer, Ronald Clifton, is knowledge and helpfulness personified. To find out more about the wide range of services they offer, contact the address above.

Public Record Office,
Kew,
Richmond,
Surrey.
TW9 4DU

Tel: 0181 876 3444
Fax: 0181 878 8905
Web site: www.pro.gov.uk

With 96 miles of shelving, the Public Record Office is an overwhelmingly valuable national resource. For those interested in Great War research there is a veritable goldmine: Service Records, Medal Rolls, Pension Records, War Diaries, Trench Maps and much more.

Ministry of Defence,
CS (RM) 2b,
Bourne Avenue,
Hayes,
Middlesex.
UB3 1RF

Tel: 0181 573 3831
Fax: 0181 573 3831

Until recently the records of service of both officers and other ranks were all held by the Ministry of Defence. This situation is changing and eventually all surviving records will be available to view with the Public Record Office (PRO). At the moment, however, the PRO may not have the records of a particular soldier. The Ministry of Defence cannot guarantee that they will be able to find the records a researcher may require and warn that the majority were destroyed by enemy action in 1940.

The Imperial War Museum,
Lambeth Road,
London.
SE1 6HZ

Tel: 0171 416 5000
Fax: 0171 416 5374

Web site: www.iwm.org.uk

The Imperial War Museum is an important resource for research. The staff at the Department of Printed Books (books@iwm.org.uk) and the Photographic Archive (photos@iwm.org.uk) are extremely helpful. The Museum offers many services, and the Great War exhibits and displays in the museum building are fascinating.

The Army Museums Ogilby Trust,
No 2 St Thomas Centre,
Southgate Street,
Winchester.
SO23 9EF

The trust holds lists of the holdings of many regimental museums.

The Somme Association,
Somme Heritage Centre,
Craigavon House,
Circular Road,
Belfast.
BT4 2NA

The Somme Association specialises in the records of individual units and soldiers, especially of Irish Units and Irishmen in other units.

EDITOR'S ACKNOWLEDGEMENTS

THE Imperial War Museum. In particular, Christopher Hunt, Deputy Keeper, Department of Printed Books; Shetland Archives. In particular, Brian Smith for help and advice; Shetland Library; The Commonwealth War Graves Commission. In particular, Peter Francis, Media & PR Co-ordinator; The Public Records Office; The Western Front Association. In particular, Ronald Clifton, Historical Information Officer; Sandy Cluness; Jim Moncrieff; John J. Graham; Ray Westlake Military Books; Sunset Militaria; Louise Bishop; The Regimental Museum of the Queen's Own Highlanders (Seaforth and Camerons), Seaforth Highlanders and The Queen's Own Highlanders, Fort George, Inverness-shire; Charlotte Black; Beatrice Nisbet.

ABOUT THE EDITOR

ALEX Cluness was born in 1969. He went to the Anderson High School and the University of Aberdeen. On returning to Shetland he taught history and then English at the Anderson for several years. His poetry has been published in *New Writing Scotland*, *The Edinburgh Review* and *Northwords*. He has also contributed both poetry and prose to local volumes. He is the joint-editor of *The New Shetlander* and a trustee of The Shetland Arts Trust. He is working on a book, *The Boys: Shetland Soldiers of the Great War*.

His grandfather, A. J. Cluness, served with the 1st Gordon Highlanders in the First World War.

BIBLIOGRAPHY

Ackroyd, Peter, *Hawksmoor*, Penguin, London, 1993.

Barker, Pat, *Regeneration*, Penguin, London, 1992.

Blake, Robert, ed. *The Private Papers of Douglas Haig 1914-1919*, Eyre & Spottiswoode, London, 1952.

Brown, Malcolm, *The Imperial War Museum Book of the Western Front*, Sidgwick & Jackson in Association with the Imperial War Museum, London, 1993.

Chapman, Guy, *A Passionate Prodigality*, Ashford, Buchan & Enright, London, Leatherhead, 1990.

Coppard, George, *With Machine Gun to Cambrai*, Papermac, London, 1986.

DeGroot, Gerald J., *Blighty: British Society in the Era of the Great War*, Longman, London, 1996.

Dyer, Geoff, *The Missing of the Somme*, Penguin, London, 1995.

Fussell, Paul, *The Great War and Modern Memory*, Oxford University Press, London, 1977.

Gilbert, Martin, *First World War*, Weidenfeld and Nicolson, London, 1994.

Glover, Jon and Silkin, Jon, eds. *The Penguin Book of First World War Prose*, Penguin, London, 1990.

Hay, Ian, *The First Hundred Thousand*, Richard Drew, Glasgow, 1985.

Hiscock, Eric, *The Bells of Hell Go Ting a Ling a Ling*, Corgi, London, 1977.

Horne, Alistair, *The Price of Glory: Verdun 1916*, Penguin, London, 1993.

James, Brig. E.A., O.B.E., T.D., *British Regiments 1914-1918*, Naval Military Press, London, 1993.

Johnson, J.H., *Stalemate! The Great Trench Warfare Battles of 1915-1917*, Arms and Armour, London, 1995.

Jünger, Ernst, *The Storm of Steel*, Constable, London, 1994.

Keegan, John, *The Face of Battle*, Pimlico, London, 1994.

Livesey, Anthony, *The Viking Atlas of World War One*, Viking, London, 1994.

Macdonald, Lyn, *They Called It Passchendaele: The Story of the Third Battle of Ypres and of the men who fought in it*, Penguin, London, 1993.

Macdonald, Lyn, *Somme*, Penguin, London, 1993.

Manning, *The Middle Parts of Fortune*, Granada, 1977.

Manson, Thomas, *Shetland's Roll of Honour and Roll of Service*, T & J Manson, Lerwick, 1920.

McCarthy, Chris, *Passchendaele: The Day-by-Day Account*, Arms and Armour, London, 1995.

McCarthy, Chris, *The Somme: The Day-by-Day Account*, Arms & Armour, 1995.

McPhail, Helen, *Wilfred Owen: Poet and Soldier*, Gliddon Books in Association with the Wilfred Owen Association, 1993.

Middlebrook, Martin, *The Kaiser's Battle*, Penguin, London, 1983.

Nicholls, Jonathan, *Cheerful Sacrifice: The Battle of Arras 1917*, Leo Cooper, London, 1995.

Remarque, Erich Maria, *All Quiet on the Western Front*, Putnam, London, 1929.

Royle, Trevor, ed. *In Flanders Fields: Scottish Poetry and Prose of The First World War*, Mainstream, Edinburgh, 1990.

Sassoon, Siegfried, *The War Poems*, Faber, London, 1983.

Silkin, Jon, ed., *The Penguin Book of First World War Poetry*, Penguin, London, 1988.

Simpson, Andy, *Hot Blood & Cold Steel*, Tom Donovan, 1993.

Sutherland, Capt. D, M.C., T.D. *War Diary of the Fifth Seaforth Highlanders*, The Bodley Head, London, 1920.

Treves, Sir Frederick, ed. *Made in the Trenches*, George Allen & Unwin, London, November 1916.

Warner, Philip, *Passchendaele: The Story Behind the Tragic Victory of 1917*, Sidgwick & Jackson, London, 1988.

Winter, Denis, *Death's Men*, Penguin, London, 1979.

Winter, Denis, *Haig's Command*, Penguin, London, 1991.

Wolff, Leon, *In Flanders Fields*, Penguin, London, 1979.